WITNESS

*The Historical Visit of President Muse Bihi Abdi
to the United States of America*

March 13-25, 2022

Jama Musse Jama

Washington D.C. - Hargeysa

*I am proud of the Somaliland people
for how resilient they are*
Muse Bihi Abdi, 2022
March 14th

*We are not economically strong, we
are not military strong, we are poor,
but we are very proud, and we
make our decisions on our own and
no one can influence us.*
Muse Bihi Abdi, 2022
March 15th

REDSEA-ONLINE Cultural Foundation
Fidiyaha Aqoonta iyo Ereyga Dhigan – Xarunta dhexe
Daarta Oriental Hotel - Hargeysa, Somaliland
Telephone: 00 252 2 525109 - Email: bookshop@redsea-online.com

Copyright © Jama Musse Jama, 2023
Published by Ponte Invisibile (redsea-online), 2023, Hargeysa

Inquiries to the editor
Via Pietro Giordani 4, 56123 Pisa, Italy
www.ponteinvisibile.com
email: editor@redsea-online.com | editor@ponteinvisibile.com

Copyright © Ponte Invisibile Edizioni 2023
A REDSEA-ONLINE Publishing Group Company.

ISBN 978-88-88934-75-4
EAN 9788888934754

Internal and cover design:
SAGALJET (info@sagaljet.net), Hargeysa, Somaliland.

A catalogue record for this book is available from the Hargeysa Cultural Centre Library (HCCL) Classification system: (check on redsea-online.org/boss)

Jama Musse Jama / *Witness: The Historical Visit of President Muse Bihi Abdi to the United States of America* / 160 pp / cm. 14x17 / 2022

To the wider Somaliland youth, who are eagerly waiting the Day of International Recognition of their country.

CONTENTS

List of abbreviations

AFRICOM	Africa Command
AU	African Union
CCF	Cheetah Conservation Foundation
CPC	CPC (*Taiwan Chines Petroleum*)
DoD	Department of Defence
GDP	Growth Domestic Product
GW	George Washington University
ICCF	International Conservation Caucus Foundation
ICG	International Crisis Group
IGAD	Intergovernmental Authority on Development
IFC	International Finance Corporation
ITA	International Trade Administration
MIGA	Multilateral Investment Guarantee Agency
NED	National Endowment for Democracy
NSC	National Security Council
SLPA	Somaliland Professionals of America
SNM	Somali National Movement
UN	United Nations
USAID	U.S. Agency for International Development
VOA	Voice of America
WINEP	Washington Institute for Near East Policy
WB	World Bank

Acknowledgment

Eventful and decisive moments like a mission from an unrecognized country to the United States of America is not something that comes as an easy arrangement. They are the results of a long-standing effort and determined personality in the leadership and team they build. That is why I want to acknowledge the leadership of the Somaliland Mission in the USA especially Mr. Bashir Goth who has done an incredible job to make the visit a reality and a seed for fruitful partnership between the two nations. This happened within a general new policy of Somaliland Foreign Affairs under the leadership of Dr Essa Kayd, the Minister. The Office of the President and his General Secretory, Mr. Mubarak Taani was very helpful in facilitating getting copies of the documents used in this book as well as some of the original photos. I would like also to acknowledge and express gratitude to all the delegation team members who have represented the people and presented the voices of Somaliland eloquently in all the different places within the mission. Above all, it is my heartfelt gratitude to my president H.E. Muse Bihi Abdi who gave me the chance to be part of this historical mission and gave me the chance to be a small part in the wider impactful purposeful mission we had. Of course, it will be of unethical not to state the determinantal role of the institutions and individuals from the USA side who have made the visit possible and informative for both sides. Acknowledgments are not an easy put as there are so many to be grateful for and space and time will not allow mentioning all. Hence, grateful to everyone who has made the mission, this small taken of the historical mission of Somaliland President Muse Bihi Abdi.

Introduction

Between the 13th and 25th of March 2022, I had the privilege of being a member of the Somaliland Delegation led by the President of the Republic, HE Muse Bihi Abdi, to the United States of America. My official position as Senior European Affairs Advisor to the President provided me the opportunity to support my country to a degree that outshone even my longstanding civil society role in Somaliland's nation-building process. The visit represented a turning point in the history of relations between Somaliland and America, and its significance and outcomes have provided much to reflect upon, as this contribution hopes to do. The first part of this book contains my reflections on this US trip. The second part contains geopolitics documents on Somaliland recognition.

The nature of the US delegation was unique, tailored appropriately to gain as much as possible from this trip, and consisting of two major groups. The first group, led by the President, and including five cabinet ministers and two senior advisors, embodied the political voice of the Republic of Somaliland. The second group brought together the interests of the business community and economic sector of the country and included leaders of major wealth-generating companies from the country and beyond.

This was the first visit of Muse Bihi to the United States as an incumbent president, and the latest of any sitting Somaliland leader since President Ahmed Mahamed Mahamoud "Silaanyo" visited Washington, D.C. from the 22nd to the 27th of April, 2013. Prior to this, only the tour of President Mohamed Ibrahim Egal to the US in 1999 had been achieved. In neither of these earlier visits was there any direct engagement with the US government. The strong public interest in President Bihi's trip, amplified by the extensive use of social media among Somalilanders and the expectation of concrete results, meant that hopes were much higher than for previous trips. The delegation, aware of these expectations, tailored pragmatic milestones to carefully selected priorities. The key message relayed to both the Somaliland audience and to the American public, government and policy community counterparts was simple and clear: Somaliland has come to Washington not to ask for favours, but to seek meaningful engagement and partnership with the United States. The aim was to conduct constructive senior-level meetings with Biden's Administration, so as to advance a framework for sustained cooperation in a range of areas where the two countries have mutual interests.

Our goal was also to secure strong support from the U.S. Congress, by expanding the network of lawmakers from both parties who would actively work to advance closer relations between the countries. In addition, in order to build support for Somaliland among the wider American public, the delegation shared Somaliland's story through public events, media interviews and press appearances. The core message was to reaffirm Somaliland's commitment to advance democracy, and to advocate for resources as the building blocks of democratic society, including support for wider political inclusion, women's active participation in governance, and commitments for upcoming elections.

Another major objective was to highlight the challenges posed by the State Department's current unreasonable blanket ('Somalia'-wide) travel advisory, which is a major hurdle to attracting investment and developing Somaliland economically. This is underlined by the lack of direct U.S. government assistance to the Somaliland government, and the absence of a U.S. diplomatic presence in Hargeysa, the Capital. Finally, to stimulate business and investors' interest in Somaliland, the delegation opened dialogues with major stakeholders from global financial institutions. The mission carefully selected the key partners to meet for each area of interest.

Among the major institutions engaged by the political wing of the delegation were the Biden Administration, State Department, Department of Defence, National Security Council (NSC), members of the House and Senate from both parties, USAID, AFRICOM, National Endowment for Democracy (NED) and United Nations (UN). For its business engagement, the mission met various World Bank agencies, including the International Finance Corporation (IFC), as well as U.S. trade promotion organs, including the International Trade Administration (ITA), U.S. Commercial Service, Multilateral Investment Guarantee Agency (MIGA) and the Chamber of Commerce, to explore possible avenues for investment and trade.

To maximize the impact of the visit on American public opinion towards the case of Somaliland, the president addressed, as keynote speaker, the very influential Heritage Foundation.[1] He also gave speeches at leading American universities, including George Washington University (GWU), and think tanks, such as the Washington Institute for Near East Policy (WINAP). Other members of the delegation appeared at public events arranged by counterpart institutions on environment, wildlife, and people-to-people connections.

Tremendous progress was made on all objectives, augmented by a number of concrete commitments secured at the end of the mission. Assistant Secretary of State for African Affairs, Molly Phee, led the team from the Biden Administration who met the delegation. The Administration identified specific areas for collaboration

---

[1] The Heritage Foundation is a conservative think tank based in Washington D.C. In October 2021, it published a report entitled "The U.S. Should Recognize Somaliland," making a strong case for Somaliland's recognition by the U.S. as a sovereign nation. See the report at: www.heritage.org.

that reflected a policy shift towards engagement, with the National Security Council notably agreeing to President Bihi's proposal to create working groups to advance collaboration across a number of priority areas. The DoD, for its part, expressed interest in a Berbera port visit from U.S. Navy vessels. The State Department suggested five areas of closer collaboration, including maritime security, counterterrorism, environmental protection, humanitarian assistance and business promotion. From the political side, a bipartisan cohort from amongst the House of Representatives dispatched a letter to the Biden Administration advocating for deeper engagement on shared diplomatic, economic and security interests. They also agreed to the introduction of legislation calling for US recognition of Somaliland[2], whereas several Somaliland allies in the Senate put forward a bipartisan Somaliland Partnership Act, which called for more direct, government-to-government engagement with Somaliland. The Act reflected "the sense of Congress that a stronger relationship between the United States and Somaliland would provide numerous, mutually beneficial, strategic opportunities due to Somaliland's geographic location in the Horn of Africa and next to the Gulf of Aden; democratic credentials, including peaceful transfers of power following elections".[3] The influential Heritage Foundation unapologetically endorsed Somaliland's full recognition, and Somaliland generally received

---

[2] See Appendix 3 for the full text of the letter.
[3] See Appendix 2 for the full text of the proposed bill.

engagement and public endorsement by a range of policy experts and former government officials, representing another notable achievement. Taken together, these achievements certainly constitute a marked advancement of American public awareness towards the Somaliland political and social case.

The following sections of this note present my own reflections and judgements of the meetings I directly attended, as well as those meetings that were discussed in the debrief afterwards. It also contains a commentary (again my own personal reflections) on the different speeches the President delivered at the different venues, including the political address and keynote speeches for academic and think tank audiences, as well as for the Somaliland community. In section two, I present a list of short overviews of the delegation's position of specific current issues relevant to Somaliland, including those on the region and wider global politics. In section three I discuss in more detail the nature of the mission, the structure of the delegation and the major meetings attended. I go on to summarise the successes already achieved, and then lay on the next steps and areas of follow-up, both in the immediate term and long term, to obtain tangible outcomes from the discussed points. In section four I present unedited text of the keynote speeches of the President for historical documentation. As per the appendix, the book contains a selected list of news items and reflections of the media on the mission, and we conclude with a selection of suggested reading material on the political history of Somaliland, and more broadly on Somaliland case for self-determination.

Overview of major topics

In this chapter we summarise the position of the president and his delegation on major topics of relevance to diplomatic conversations regarding Somaliland. In many cases, the sentences are taken directly from the president's talking points in keynotes or his answers to the questions from the audience. In other cases, the concept has been reworded based on the discussion and further reflections with members of the delegation.

On Somaliland

The Republic of Somaliland is a sovereign state in the Horn of Africa that shares its borders with the Republic of Djibouti to the northwest, Federal Republic of Ethiopia to the south and west, and Federal Republic of Somalia to the east. Formerly a British Protectorate, Somaliland achieved full independence from the United Kingdom in 1960 and united with the former Italian Trusteeship of Somalia to create the Somali Republic. Somaliland subsequently reclaimed its independence in 1991 and is celebrating over three decades of vibrant democracy, territorial security and a growing economy.

On the Mission

All with all other official diplomatic visits by the President or high-level delegations, Somaliland's recognition as an independent sovereign nation shaped all of our priorities. However, making the most of the opportunity equally meant exploring all opportunities for intergovernmental and business engagement. With this in mind, the delegation expressed its willingness to take a pragmatic approach, to avoid the politically contentious issue of Somaliland's status becoming hurdle to opening a dialogue.

On China

China has become a major player in the Horn of Africa, and Somaliland aims to have good relations with all those nations working to develop and improve our region. Somaliland extends a peaceful hand of collaboration to everyone, because we know from experience what conflict means. However, we are committed to our freedom to choose who to talk to and who to collaborate with, and will not sell out these principles for any rewards or as the result of any coercion. China needs us, we need them, and we would like to have good relations, free of any ill-will.

On Taiwan

Taiwan and Somaliland are thousands of miles apart, but we share a deep-seated love of freedom and democracy. Our shared lack of recognition gives us common cause, and our shared experience learning to survive and thrive under such conditions mean we have a lot to learn from each other and a lot of reason to support each other. In particular, as the younger party in this partnership, Somaliland hopes to learn how to overcome the barriers of recognition to achieve strong development in technology and wealth generation, two areas that would greatly benefit our people.

On the US travel advisory

As a tangible step forward, the State Department should review its current travel advice to American citizens who want to visit Somaliland. The current situation, with its blanket policy which fails to distinguish Somaliland from Somalia, not only fails to do justice to Somaliland's achievements in peace and security, but consequently also hinders prospective investment and punishes over 20,000 American citizens who are either from Somaliland or have family ties to the country. A fairer policy more reflective of Somaliland's unique, separate status would make it much easier for these individuals to visit their relatives and, more importantly, to invest across all sectors of the economy.

On the impossibility of reunification with Somalia

Somaliland is an independent, sovereign state and its people and government will not negotiate on reunification. Somaliland agreed to enter into talks with Somalia to both establish formal bilateral relations as two neighbouring independent nations, and to put an end to any ill-will arising from past atrocities and from Somaliland's legal decision to dissolve the union. These attempts at dialogue on the bases of two independent, sovereign governments failed because Somalia has repeatedly displayed no desire to engage in constructive negotiation. The political and security situation in

Somalia continues to deteriorate, while Somaliland has built a functioning, stable and democratic state with the institutions and capabilities necessary to engage with foreign governments as an independent nation. We look forward to a new U.S. strategy towards Somaliland that acknowledges these fundamental differences and includes direct cooperation with our government. This change in policy would not involve a break with the *status quo* on the ground, but instead a recognition of the *status quo*: Somaliland and Somalia function completely separately, and the sooner this is recognised, the sooner that unnecessary, self-defeating barriers against engagement with Somaliland are eased.

On Somaliland-Somalia talks

After a decade of fruitless attempts at dialogue, Somaliland sees no conceivable value in the continuation of discussions between Somaliland and Somalia. Somalia refuses to acknowledge the democratic will of the Somaliland people, as expressed in both elections and a 2001 referendum, and we will not remain hostage to their intransigence. Somaliland remains prepared to pursue all available avenues for its international recognition, which, in the present circumstances, the international community has a moral obligation to support. Somaliland strived with great effort and success over the past 31 years to achieve peace and stability in a troubled Horn of Africa region, and we see a promising future regardless of Somaliland's status. However, international recognition would undoubtedly unlock foreign aid and access to international lenders like the World Bank, while also allowing us to conduct international business without the oppressive obstacles we now face. Widespread and severe youth unemployment, lack of progress on recognition and delayed economic development threaten to undermine our democracy. It's hard to convince someone who has voted in three elections but never had a job that democracy is still the right path.

On lack of recognition

Lack of recognition has held Somaliland back, and we have had to work twice as hard to achieve the democratic and security successes that we have made. Meanwhile, lack of recognition continues to tie us to the fate of Somalia, who remain unable to overcome the chaos that has endured there for 30 years, and this captivity and distraction impedes Somaliland's ability to both serve as a stabilizing force in the region, as well as from fulfilling the aspiration of our citizens. On bilateral level, Somaliland cannot enter into direct agreements with other nations, which makes formal cooperation and assistance virtually impossible. Practically, we are subject to a variety of international restrictions and advisories that apply to Somalia due to the terrorist presence and instability there, but have little relevance to the situation on the ground in Somaliland. Instead, they simply serve to impede our further development and growth.

On the fear of being first to recognise Somaliland

For the past 31 years, every country was happy to acknowledge and praise Somaliland's stability and institutional development, but is reluctant to be the first country to recognize our independence. While being the first to do so might impose some small diplomatic risk or cost, this is nothing compared to the long-term risks and costs that would come with failing to seize the opportunity to solidify Somaliland's status and role in the region. Indeed, Somaliland's ability police terror, human trafficking, piracy and organised crime on its territory on behalf of the international community has reduced costs and risks for the U.S., and ensuring Somaliland's continued thriving is thus an easy win for the U.S. as global challenges grow elsewhere.

On regional economic integration

Somaliland has expanded trade and economic cooperation with neighbouring countries, from Ethiopia and Djibouti to Kenya. The rehabilitation of the Berbera Port and the infrastructural revitalisation of the Berbera Corridor will allow Somaliland to serve as a key trade and logistics node in a more fully integrated region. Cooperation between Somaliland and Somalia will not come about by trying to force the former back into union with the latter, but through accepting the reality of Somaliland's independence, and then supporting Somaliland in promoting regional economic integration with all its neighbours.

On African Union

An African Union (AU) fact-finding mission in 2005 concluded that the Somaliland case was "unique and self-justified in African political history" and that "the case [for recognition] should not be linked to the notion of 'opening a pandora's box'" of further fragmentation of other African states. The fact-finding mission recommended that the AU "should find a special method of dealing with this outstanding case" as soon as possible. The President's repeated reference of this during the visit underlies its continued relevance, even as he held out little hope of the AU acting on these recommendations given its current structure. The U.S. could use its diplomatic leverage to find African backers who might place this on the agenda of the AU for future debate, however.

On the Red Sea and Bab el-Mandeb Strait

Somaliland's contribution to maritime security and trade in this critical region are more important than ever. Somaliland is responsible for about 38% of the Red Sea (the entire Gulf of Aden), and is located about 70 miles from the heart of the Bab el-Mandeb Straight, and this critical responsibility at a time of instability in the Red Sea region means that Somaliland can no longer be left out of discussion on how these waterways are to be governed. The Red Sea can be an entry point of the conversation with U.S. and others with an interest in the area's security and stability, including when it comes to commercial interests and trade around these key commercial chokepoints.

On the Horn of Africa, China and other Superpowers

Superpower competition over the Horn of Africa has grown dramatically over the past decade. Major players such as China, the U.S., UK, Russia, Saudi Arabia and Qatar are all vying for influence over all countries in the region, whether in terms of diplomatic, security or commercial interests. China has reached out to Somaliland, although our divergent views on Somaliland's engagement with Taiwan has hindered the opportunity for cooperation. China's pressure to cut off ties with Taiwan was not well received in Hargeysa, as was captured in this defiant statement made by President Bihi during his tour of the U.S.: "We are not economically strong, we are not military strong, we are poor, but we are very proud, and we make our decisions on our own and no one can influence us."

On U.S. collaboration

Somaliland seeks partnership with the U.S. across a number of priority areas: security (intelligence, coast guard capacitation, training); investment in natural resources (minerals and oil); contribution to the development of the Berbera Corridor; support for elections and democratic processes; and direct aid via USAID and other USA channels focusing on climate change, environment, water and agriculture. On the diplomatic front, Somaliland believes that effective bilateral relations in the short term can be achieved with U.S. representation in Hargeysa, on par with governments such as Ethiopia or the U.K., as well as through the revival of the "dual track policy" that distinguishes Somaliland from Somalia. Ultimately, Somaliland seeks U.S. leadership on matters of recognition of its independent status. Unlike the U.S.'s support for the peaceful separation of South Sudan and Sudan, the legal basis for Somaliland's independence requires no alteration of colonial borders, and no messy politics of secession, as Somaliland is already functionally separate and run by a civilian government not a rebel movement.

On U.S. presence in a fully recognized Somaliland

A strong American presence in an independent Somaliland would be a hedge against Beijing's growing influence in Djibouti, which includes a well-equipped army base near the Ethiopia-Djibouti Railway. In Somaliland, the near refurbishment of the Berbera Corridor will provide an alternative route between the Gulf of Aden and Ethiopia, thus linking any future military cooperation operating out of Somaliland fully integrated into the wider Horn of Africa theatre.

Historical background of Somaliland

Somaliland became an independent, sovereign state on 26 June 1960 - an achievement acknowledged by all five permanent members of the United Nations Security Council and many other governments (Jama Musse, 2017). Five days after this independence, Somaliland united with Somalia with the aim of creating a "Greater Somalia," bringing together all people of ethnic Somali origin spread across five former colonial territories in the Horn of Africa. Almost immediately, Somalilanders were excluded from decision-making and representative governance in the new Somali Republic, and disenchantment with this arrangement continued throughout the early years of the union, as their political and economic isolation only grew (Further reading to 'Somaliland: A political history', Jama Musse, 2017).

After assuming power over the leadership of the Somali Republic in a military coup in October 1969, Mohamed Siad Barre soon transformed the country into a military dictatorship marked by widespread human rights abuses. The growing discontent with Siad Barre's oppressive leadership led to extensive opposition in Somaliland, to which the Barre regime responded with a brutal military campaign of suppression that killed an estimated 50,000 Somaliland civilians and displaced an estimated 500,000 others as refugees across neighbouring countries and beyond. "Hargeysa and Burco were ghost towns, with only the Somali National Army in residence. There was nothing left to administer, and nobody left to govern" (Renders, 2012). The army became isolated. SNM increasingly got backing through tribal elders' ability to get local clans to support and the diaspora. By the time of Siad Barre's eventual downfall in 1991, the main cities of Hargeysa and Burao had been reduced to rubble. With the collapse of the Somali state that year, Somaliland withdrew from the union it had voluntarily entered in 1960 and reaffirmed its independent sovereign status, based on the borders of the former British Somaliland Protectorate (Jama Musse, 2017; Walls, 2014; Jhazbhay, 2009; Bradbury, 2008).

From 1991 to today, Somaliland has come a long way, establishing the institutions and practices of self-governance and, as a result, taking control over its own destiny. 2022 marks 31 years since the lawful dissolution of the failed Somali union, meaning that the Somaliland people have spent more time independent than under the three decades as part of Somalia. After so long, it is high time that the international community takes action to recognise this reality once and for all, something that the International Crises Group (ICG) has called for. As its 2016 report argues, "The African Union (AU) needs to engage in preventive diplomacy now, laying the groundwork for resolution of the dispute before it becomes a confrontation from which either side views violence as the only exit." (ICG, 2016).

African Union sent a fact-finding mission to Somaliland from 30 April to 4th May 2005, to see "the prevailing situation (political, socio-economic, security, humanitarian and other related issues) in the country and listen to the concerns of the leadership and people of Somaliland." The same message at every place, from interior cities to the capital, and from every block of the society was *"the Irreversible independence of Somaliland; the irreversible sovereignty of Somaliland; no return to the Union with Somalia; the quest for recognition from the AU and the international community"*. The overall assessment of the mission was that there was an evident conviction and emotion among the Somalilanders that Somaliland *"has all the attributes of an independent sovereign State, which they [Somalilanders] say the international community should objectively consider."* The mission outlined in its recommendations that "The lack of recognition ties the hands of the authorities and people of Somaliland as they cannot effectively and sustainably transact with the outside to pursue the reconstruction and development goals." It also called the AU should be disposed to judge the case of Somaliland from an objective historical viewpoint and a moral angle vis-a-vis the aspirations of the people. Finally, the mission recognized that the fact that the union between Somaliland and Somalia was never ratified and malfunctioned when it went into went into action from 1960 to 1990, *"makes Somaliland's search for recognition historically unique and self-justified in African political history."* Objectively viewed, the report says *"the case should not be linked to the notion of "opening a Pandora's box". As such, the AU should find a special method of dealing with this outstanding case."* (See AU, 2005).

While the AU is certainly the optimal forum for addressing the issue of Somaliland quest for recognition, progress will only be made if major power within the international community show leadership in mobilising the body to act.

Peace and democracy as domestic political will

Somaliland's democracy is derived from a natural expression of indigenous consensus-based decision-making, traditionally rooted in nomadic intercommunal practices, where everyone has a say in the process of decision-making. This traditional principles were adapted for modern governance during the guerrilla war against the Siad Barre regime, with the Somali National Movement (SNM) introducing the concept of the *Guurti* (traditional elders whose job it was to scrutinize and ultimately approve by common assent decisions made by an appointed political leadership) into their governance structure. Following the liberation of the country by the SNM in 1991, Somaliland went about the task of institutionalizing its democracy over the course of five major internal meetings, starting with the Grand Conference of the Northern Peoples in Burao, held over six weeks, concluding with the declaration of Somaliland's independence from Somalia on 18 May

1991 (Jama Musse, 2017; Walls, 2014; Jhazbhay, 2009; Bradbury, 2008). These peace conferences were managed and financed by locals, who provided their own food and shelter. With its commitment to organically bottom-up rather than top-down processes of reconciliation and state building, peace in Somaliland was forged through a combination of community spirit and persistence, as was the socioeconomic and political recovery which has followed.

In the subsequent years, Somaliland has developed a stable, democratic system of politics, merging modern and traditional elements. In 2002, Somaliland made the transition from a clan-based system of democracy to multi-party democracy following a nation-wide popular referendum over the constitution, formalising the *Guurti* as an Upper House of Elders, which secures the support of traditional clan-based power structures. There have since been regular elections—six in total across all levels of government—and frequent turnover of power between the main political parties. The 2003 presidential election was won by Dahir Rayale Kahin by just 80 votes from among nearly half a million cast ballots, over his opponent Ahmed Mahamed Mahamoud "Silaanyo" (UNPW, 2016). The tables were turned in 2010, with Silaanyo winning 49% of the vote to his main competitor's 33%. Then, in November 2017, Muse Bihi Abdi was elected with 55% of the vote, becoming the country's fifth president, and cementing a tradition of peaceful handovers of power rare to the region (Mills et.al, 2021, Walls et. al., 2021).

Stability in a turbulent region

Since reclaiming independence in 1991, Somaliland has built a functioning, stable, democratic state in an otherwise volatile security environment, earning it the description of "the strongest democracy in the region" by the *Economist* (Nov 13th, 2017)[4]. Somaliland's governance system serves as a model for others in the Horn of Africa and beyond who seek to govern responsibly and provide opportunities for their citizens. Somaliland's nationwide one-person one-vote elections and peaceful transition of power over the last two decades have all been declared free and fair by international and local observers (See Mills et. al, 2021). In May 2021, Somaliland successfully conducted a combined parliamentary and local council election and welcomed election observers from around the world. Somaliland's capable security forces, law enforcement authorities and strong judiciary have deterred terrorism and piracy from its territory and adjacent waterways, and have enabled the arrest and prosecution of wildlife traffickers seeking to transit vulnerable animals via the country.

---

[4] See *"Why Somaliland is east Africa's strongest democracy"*, 13 November 2017, at https://www.economist.com/the-economist-explains/2017/11/13/why-somaliland-is-east-africas-strongest-democracy [retrieved 7 June 2022].

Trade and economic development

Somaliland is an emerging trade and shipping hub, with a growing consumer market that should appeal to international investors, particularly U.S. companies. The country is increasingly sought out by global investors interested in its logistics, fishery, agriculture, mineral, and infrastructure sectors, as well as its role as reliable base for expanding commercial relations throughout Africa. Somaliland is strategically located just 70 miles from the Bab el-Mandeb Strait joining the Red Sea and Gulf of Aden, a major sea lane through which 30% of the world's shipping passes. While Somaliland welcomes interest from foreign companies seeking to cultivate our local resources, their investments must also create opportunities for our citizens.

Model of success for the Horn of Africa

Somaliland has established a successful market economy, catalysed by low levels of regulation and a comparatively small government bureaucracy. The nation's thriving services sector hosts a number of major international businesses, including an indigenous international airline, a competitive telecommunications industry and a $17 million Coca Cola production facility that is a supply hub for the entire region. Leaders and experts from around the world have recognized Somaliland's commitment to democratic governance, strong rule of law, embrace of market competition, and innovative deployment of technology. Moreover, Somaliland has become an attractive area for energy exploration activities by international companies, and is capitalizing on its natural resources, including proven reserves of iron and manganese, with in tandem with private sector partners. When it comes to oil, several companies have signed production sharing agreements with the government and are involved in early-stage surveying.

Previous Somaliland presidential visits to the U.S.

Both President Mohamed Ibrahim Egal and President Ahmed Mahamed Mahamoud "Silaanyo" visited the United State during their term as incumbent. The following two paragraphs will recount in brief the formal meetings the two former presidents had with their counterpart U.S. administrations and other government bodies. It should also be noted that Somaliland's first Foreign Minister, Yusuf Ali Sheekh Madar, visited the States in 1992, as a representative of President Abdirahman Ahmed Ali "Tuur", while U.S. Assistant Secretary of State for African Affairs Dr Jendayi Elizabeth Frazer made a historic trip to Somaliland in 2007.

1999 - President Mohamed Ibrahim Egal

In 1999, President Egal visited New York and Washington, dedicating a week for each city. In Washington, the President met Assistant Secretary of State for Foreign Affairs Ms. Susan Rice and her special advisor for the Horn of Africa John Prendergast, as well as the National Security Council director for Africa Ms. Gayle Smith. While Egal succeeded in persuading, and winning support from, Smith and Prendergast, convincing them of the benefits of greater U.S. partnership with Somaliland, Rice remained inflexible on the question, aligning herself on the position with Secretary of State Albright. Egal also visited Capitol Hill, where he met Donald Payne (Dem, NJ) and Tom Campbell (Rep, Calif.). Interestingly, the President's visit to Washington coincided with the presence in Hargeysa of a US delegation comprising diplomats serving in neighbouring Djibouti, responsible for the Somaliland dossier in East Africa, as well as Ms. Arlene Ferril, then in charge of Somalia in the US State Department. During this trip, President Egal met UN Secretary-General Kofi Annan and his Undersecretary for Political Affairs, Kier Prendergast.

2013 - President Ahmed Mahamed Mahamoud "Silaanyo"

President Silaanyo" conducted a five-day visit to Washington in 2013, where he conferred with senior U.S. officials and other stakeholders on the prospects for peace and security in the Horn of Africa region. The president was accompanied by a delegation that included First Lady Amina Haji Mahammad Jirde; Hersi Ali H. Hassan, Minister of Presidential Affairs; Mohamed Abdullahi Omar, Minister of Foreign Affairs; Sa'ad Ali Shire, Minister of Planning; Hussein Abdi Dualeh, Minister of Mining, Energy, and Water Resources; and Osman Sahardiid, Minister of State for Finance. The President was invited to speak at Atlantic Council's Michael S. Ansari Africa Center, and the delegation took advantage of opportunities to meet with various U.S. officials, including Undersecretary of State Wendy Sherman, Undersecretary of State for African Affairs Donald Yamamato, USAID Deputy Administrator Donald Steinberg, and Assistant Administrator for Africa Earl W. Gast. On the security side, the Somaliland delegation convened with Assistant Secretary of Defense for Special Operations and Low Intensity Conflict Michael Sheehan, as well as Deputy Assistant Secretary of Defense for African Affairs Amanda J. Dory. The President also met with Members of Congress to offer Somaliland's perspective on recent events in the region. The President concluded his visit by meeting with Somaliland expatriates residing in the U.S.

The Mission

The nature of the mission

The mission began with an invitation by the Heritage Foundation, a leading think tank with a Republican political orientation, to address a select audience on Somaliland's quest for recognition. In attendance were scholars, policymakers, senators, congressmen, journalists, members of civil society, and experts on American policy towards Africa. From there, over the course of a tightly-packed 20-day schedule, the delegation held substantial face-to-face meetings with a diverse array of counterparts. Among the senior officials of Biden administration met, there were representatives from the State Department, Department of Defence, AFRICOM, USAID and National Security Council. The delegation also had the chance to meet with international organizations and independent U.S. bodies, such as the UN, World Bank, International Finance Corporation, Multilateral Investment Guarantee Agency, U.S. Commercial Service, U.S. Chamber of Commerce, National Endowment for Democracy, International Trade Administration, International Conservation Caucus Foundation, and Cheetah Conversation Fund. American officials, without exception, applauded Somaliland for its extraordinary achievements in building a democratic, self-sufficient state, while voicing recognition of the importance of Somaliland and America's shared values and goals fort the region.

Moreover, the President had the opportunity to address scholars and researchers of two major academic and policy institutions of the country, George Washington University and the Washington Institute for Near East Policy, in both cases with a keynote speech followed by lively discussion and Q&A sessions. These in-person academic discussions also allowed for substantial virtual attendance from all over the world, and the online audience had an opportunity to ask questions. The delegation also attended an international conference on Somaliland, organized by Somaliland Professional Association in collaboration with the Liaison Office for Somaliland in the U.S., including a presidential dinner where over 500 citizens attended. The President and members of the delegations met with press from major international outlets, including exclusive interviews with the. See Appendix 2 for the full list of printed and audio-visual interviews of the delegation.

Delegation structure

The Somaliland delegation led by President Bihi consisted of two major components: a political wing made up of the President, five members of his cabinet (the ministers of foreign affairs, interior, information, environment and commerce) and two senior presidential advisors (for both economic affairs and European affairs). The second component of the delegation consisted of major business leaders of the country, including those representing TELESOM, Dahabshiil Group, SomCable and Omaar company. The workplan was organized and led by the Somaliland Representative Office to the U.S.. A full list of delegation participants and their roles can be found in Appendix 1. Most of the meetings were conducted in parallel, with the Minister of Commerce and the Economic Advisor to the President attending commercially-related meetings alongside the business community, while the rest of the delegation attended meetings of political, security and government-to-government policy relevance.

Highlights of individual meetings

On the public event at the Heritage Foundation, broadcast live across social media, President Musa Bihi Abdi addressed the issue of "The Great Promise of Closer U.S.-Somaliland Ties". This address, followed by a Q&A led by Joshua Meservey, Research Fellow for Africa at the Institute, expressed the delegation's ambitions and expectations from this trip. President Bihi provided a brief overview of the history of Somaliland and its successful track record as a democratic government and a secure and functioning nation. While reiterating Somaliland's goal of a fully recognized independent Somaliland, President Bihi also formulated ways Somaliland can work with the U.S. in the short term, from its current position of non-recognition, including how the U.S can better support Somaliland. Full text of the address of President Bihi is reproduced in chapter 4 of this booklet.

Meetings with the Biden Administration were cordial and productive[5]. At the initial address, President Bihi's key message was how strengthening the partnership between U.S. and Somaliland was more vital is than ever, because of the growing challenges in the region in terms of continued instability and terrorist activities in Somalia, civil conflict in Ethiopia, growing Chinese presence in the Horn of Africa, and democratic backsliding across the region more broadly.

The Somaliland Delegation expressed encouragement with the Biden Administration's recent signs of increased interest in Somaliland, and reiterated how Somaliland can help U.S. through intelligence cooperation, access to the modernized Berbera seaport for commercial and humanitarian purposes, as well as in assisting the U.S.'s efforts to counter China's growing presence in the Horn. President Bihi also urged the U.S. Government to open new avenues of support for Somaliland, such as creating direct dialogue between the two governments, and

---

[5] The Somaliland delegation met U.S. Administration officials led by Ms. Molly Phee, Assistant Secretary of State for African Affairs at the State Department, accompanied by her Deputy Mr. Peter Lord, Mr Machel Fooks, Senior Somalia Desk Officer, Ms. Marissa Lemargie-Lavaque from Office of East African Affairs, Bureau for Africa of the USAID, Ms. Maura Barry Boyly, Senior Deputy Assistant Administrator and Interim Global Water Coordinator at USAID, as well as Ms. Ilan Goldenberg of Department of Defense and Ambassador Andrew Young, Deputy to the Commander for Civil-Military Engagement, U.S. Africa Command at the Department of Defense.

resuming special arrangements for the direct transfer of humanitarian, health and environmental assistance, as well as election funding support. The Somaliland delegation also requested revisions to the U.S. travel advisory for Somaliland that better reflect the realities on the ground, and the establishment of a U.S. diplomatic office in Hargeysa. The Administration officials welcomed all the raised points, and agreed to deepen cooperation on key shared objectives, including maritime security, counterterrorism, humanitarian assistance, environmental protection, and business promotion. The process for revision of the travel advice has been also initiated, and more frequent visits to Hargeysa by high-level U.S. officials were promised.

These broad policy commitments were subsequently fleshed out in more granular discussions with U.S. government agencies. In a meeting with National Security Council officials, Dana Banks, Deputy Assistant to the President and NSC Senior Director for Africa, noted that her office was developing a new U.S. policy toward Africa, which will certain take into consideration the merits of closer cooperation with Somaliland, based on the discussions of the visit. The NSC team confirmed their agreement with President Bihi's proposal to create working groups to advance each area identified as a shared interest (maritime security, counterterrorism, humanitarian assistance, environmental protection, and business promotion), while confirming DoD interest in a Berbera port visit from U.S. Navy vessels.

The Somaliland-American Conference in Washington DC

Co-hosted by the Somaliland Professionals of America and the Somaliland Mission to the U.S., the conference's major aim was to bring together delegates from Somaliland and stakeholders from the Somaliland diaspora to engage in critical discussions on the political, social, and economic development of Somaliland. In order to explore potential opportunities for the Diaspora to support the country's development, the conference engaged the audience across five major panels, including 1) Dynamics in the Horn of Africa vis-à-vis U.S.-Chinese competition and the unique role of Somaliland; 2) Gender and Inclusive Politics: Ensuring equitable representation of Somaliland women in politics; 3) Healthcare and Education Challenges and the Role of the Diaspora; 4) Democracy, Justice, and Freedom of Speech: The current party system and future thoughts on elections, media and conflict; and 5) Business and Job Creation. The organizers brought together over 300 attendees from the United States and Canada and engaged Somaliland's leaders and diverse members of the diaspora in discussions on topics that are key to the country's development.

Major achievements

This mission succeeded in garnering Somaliland the platform it needed to share its story and voice its interests in both the corridors of American power and amongst the U.S. public. The recognition of Somaliland as an independent sovereign nation was placed on the table by the delegation in all discussions it was afforded, and the visit helped advance the discussion forward. Various scholars and politicians, as well as ordinary American citizens, argued that an independent Somaliland would be a stable partner that has little risk of experiencing the tumult that frustrates American interests elsewhere in the volatile region of the Horn of Africa. Dr. Joshua Meservey, a Research Fellow at the Heritage Foundation, argues in an opinion piece filed after the visit, that "Somalilanders deserve the justice of having their decades-long practice of independence recognized and should be allowed to disassociate from the dysfunction of Somalia that hinders their development." Recognizing Somaliland's independence would, according to Meservey, enable the U.S. "to hedge against further deterioration of its position in Djibouti, which is under Chinese sway", and it would reward Somaliland for its sincere commitment to democracy and deliver the justice of honouring its strong and consistent aspiration for independence.

Another major achievement was the mutual understanding fostered towards the deepening of cooperation on key shared objectives, including maritime security, counterterrorism, humanitarian assistance, environmental protection, and business promotion. The fact that the National Security Council went as far as agreeing to establish joint working groups on these four areas is a major step. The willingness of the State

Department to review its travel advice on Somaliland, as well as its commitment to more frequent visits to Hargeysa by high-level U.S. officials, also represented important milestones. Such commitments have already proven substantive, with, on the 12th of May 2022, U.S. Army Gen. Stephen Townsend, head of U.S. Africa Command, led a delegation of U.S. Army officials to Somaliland. In Hargeysa, the delegation met with President Muse Bihi Abdi, before visiting Berbera "to view an airfield that U.S. Air Forces in Europe - Air Forces Africa assessed last summer." (Africom, 2022).

The bipartisan cohort from amongst the House of Representatives who dispatched a letter to the Biden Administration advocating for deeper engagement on shared diplomatic, economic and security interests was another achievement. The fact they also agreed to the introduction of legislation calling for US recognition of Somaliland, whereas several Somaliland allies in the Senate put forward a bipartisan Somaliland Partnership Act, which called for more direct, government-to-government engagement with Somaliland, made a political step forward.

On the business side, the commitment from the World Bank and other financial institutions to smoothen the way for Somaliland businesses to connect to world financial and commercial markets is a promising achievement that requires individual follow up from the companies involved. The delegation got the commitment of the World Bank agencies, U.S. trade promotion officials and the U.S. Chamber of Commerce to pursue avenues for investment and business collaboration.

Finally the encouraging promises from the United Nations for direct engagement on humanitarian and development assistance constitute positive perspective to work on.

The way forward

The Somaliland government is committed to undertaking the necessary efforts at home and abroad to achieve its people's quest for recognition as an independent sovereign nation. It is also committed to explore and pursue all pragmatic actions that might be taken to improve Somaliland's position in terms of wealth generation, health, education, and economic development. This mission to the United States of America proved to be an eye-opener for the Somaliland Government on what could be done to open doors amongst countries that are not currently ready to recognize Somaliland. To make the most of this opportune moment, the Somaliland government should consider the following actions as follow-up in the nearer term:

- Immediately move forward with the creation of the working groups on maritime security, counterterrorism, humanitarian assistance, environmental protection, and business promotion that were agreed to with the U.S. Government

- Follow up with U.S. officials regarding the travel advisory, U.S. office in Hargeysa, and the other practical requests made during the visit
- Leverage established channels of communication to express Somaliland's perspective on ongoing developments in the region, such as sanctions and embargoes on Somalia, easing the pressure of commodity inflation on the Somaliland public, etc.
- Balance Somaliland's strong support amongst Republican-leaning think tanks in the U.S. with those that have an audience among Democrats, so that Somaliland is able to cultivate a support base within Biden's policy circles. This might include the Brookings Institute, Atlantic Council, Center for American Progress, etc.
- Push for coverage on Somaliland within liberal media outlets (to balance out the conservative focus of much of Somaliland coverage) such as the *New York Times*
- Push for U.S. support for Somaliland participation in relevant international forums, including the Saudi-led Red Sea alliance and other important maritime security bodies
- Develop a follow-up work plan for the U.S. lobby group supporting Somaliland, in tandem with the Somaliland Mission to the U.S., including with regards to lobbying for support of the Somaliland Partnership Act
- Designate selected members of the Somaliland diaspora living in different U.S. states to organize

their communities to lobby their Representatives and Senators to move forward in passing the Somaliland Partnership Act

- Develop an ultimatum regarding the Somaliland-Somalia dialogue, which the U.S. and U.K. are still pushing, as a means to force them into adopting a more unilateral approach. This includes making clear Somaliland's position on the unsatisfactory nature of President Hassan Sheikh's proposal of Sheikh Sharif as responsible for leading the talks.
- Improving public diplomacy at home in Somaliland on the achievements of this visit, so as to demonstrate the progress made by the Bihi administration on matters of foreign policy
- Stay informed on developing public discussions in the U.S. on the Taiwan issue, so that Somaliland can continue to leverage its close relations with Taiwan

UK House of Commons: Somaliland Recognition

The UK parliament hosted a debate on 18th of January 2022 about the political recognition of Somaliland as a sovereign state. The debate was organized and led by the Rt Honourable Gavin Williamson MP, a Member of Parliament for South Staffordshire since 2010. He is Former Secretary of State for Education of the United Kingdom, who visited Somaliland in 2019 when he was serving as the UK Secretary of State for Defence. The debate was well attended by 20 MPs from all sides of the House. Chris Heaton-Harris, UK Minister for Europe from the ruling Conservative party represented the government in absence Vicky Ford, the Minister for Africa who was traveling in that week in East Africa. Following are four points of personal reflection on the nature of the debate and the possible consequences of this initiative for Somaliland recognition.

The nature of the debate

Firstly, we need to understand how the House of Commons works and where the Rt Hon Gavin Williamson's political acumen when he called for the meeting, and who else was backing him in the debate. The well-crafted initiative, leadership, consistency, and commitment of MP Williamson was extremely important in this debate, but it should also be recognized that this was not just a debate called by a single MP. It was a well-organized and coordinated session, that brought the discussion to a level that was informative about the status and highlighted the aspirations of Somaliland with regard to recognition of it as an independent state. It was also the culmination of many years of activism from MPs, and most particularly from members of the UK All-Party Parliamentary Group for Somaliland.

The All-Party Parliamentary Groups (APPG) for Somaliland was established in November 2016 with the following aim: "To promote understanding of and support for Somaliland's achievements in building peace, democratic governance and a sovereign state in the Horn of Africa". The aims also include championing "the need for continued UK assistance for Somaliland's development". An APPG is an informal, cross-party group formed by MPs and Members of the House of Lords who share a common interest, but they have no formal power or status within the Parliament. Almost all the active members of the APPG were present: Clive Betts from Sheffield; Stephen Doughty from Cardiff; Kerry McCarthy from Bristol; Matthew Offord from Hendon; and Ruth Jones from Newport West. These MPs and colleagues from the House of Lords come from different political colours: Labour, Conservative and so on, but they share their support for the Somaliland case.

The second group that should be named and recognized for their incredible contribution is Somalilanders in the UK, or British Somalilanders, the Somaliland Community, who in such a short time campaigned and contacted their

MPs but also worked hard in the social media to make the case for debate so strongly in public opinion forums. They showed that their voice counted and that is because of their unity.

The third group is the Somaliland Government, represented by its Permanent Resident's Office here in London who did marvellous job of contacting community members and promoting to tune in and follow the debate closely by calling their local MPs. When I say the Government, I do not mean only the Executive. We were all pleased, for instance, by the swift reaction from the Somaliland House of Representatives, who reacted positively and, on behalf of the people of Somaliland, thanked the UK MPs who initiated the debate.

What happened in the house?

The second question worth answering is what actually happened in the House? This was a genuine debate in which parliamentarians shaped the discourse with enthusiasm, truthfulness and excellent interventions based on facts. It is not common to involve so many MPs - more than 20 - who joined the debate and echoed the Rt Hon Gavin Williamson's strong message. There was a real convergence of minds which is uncommon in parliamentary debates.

The central message was not only the fact that Somaliland Recognition has a solid, proven legal basis, but it also has a legitimate basis in human rights. Indeed, the world owes Somaliland respect because the aspiration to become an independent state is the fundamental human right of self-determination. MPs also used the verifiable fact, that Somaliland is a reliable, credible, and democratic partner, with whom the UK can do business. This is a key point: recognising Somaliland was framed as an invitation to British businesses and viable investors to engage with Somaliland. To put their money where they are sure they can make mutual profits and achieve benefit for both the UK and Somaliland. In additional, this should be linked to the recent CDC Group investment in Berbera Port via DP World. Finally, they talked about the fundamental relationship between the United Kingdom and Somaliland; not only the historical one that many people readily cite, but also the fact that we share a future together, as so many British-Somalilanders today are rewriting the reality of this relationship with a positive new chapter. Somaliland, they told the world, is the only stable and credible spot in the turbulent and unstable Greater Horn of Africa region, and it occupies in incredibly strategic position for the Red Sea near Babel Mandeb passage.

Of course, we must recall the not-so-positive reaction of the Foreign Commonwealth and Development Office (FCDO), which maintained, as expected, the official position of successive UK governments on the issue of the recognition of Somaliland. That is the UK Government consider Somaliland recognition as a matter for Somaliland and the Federal.

Government of Somalia to agree between themselves in the first instance. This position was strongly rejected by the speakers in the debate, reminding the FCDO that this view from the junior Minister is not representative of the views of many within both the Government and the Opposition, as evidenced by the debate itself. Hon. Rushunara Ali, UK MP responded to the government position stating how the UK government took leadership role and supported Bangladesh independence when it was fighting with Pakistan, and UK did not say Bangladesh sovereignty has to be negotiated between Bangladesh and Pakistan".

But for me, I noted the following four key points in particular:

- Firstly, the counter point to the main argument of many speakers, namely reservations expressed against Somaliland recognition, were pre-emptively and comprehensively rebutted by MPs. They were unequivocal and overwhelming in their support. The work done by the community also cannot and should not be underestimated in this regard.
- Secondly, the ideas that recognising Somaliland will destabilise Somalia or that negotiations with Somalia are a viable route to recognition, were also resoundingly challenged. This is what Somaliland has always advocated, but the fact it is now being said by many UK MPs is highly significant.
- Thirdly, the MPs proposed practical steps towards common interest, for example, upgrading the status

of the UK Liaison office in Hargeysa to issue passports to British Somalilanders and travel visa to Somaliland people, as well as British Council services, that today it is unconscionable, these citizens must travel to Ethiopia.

- Finally, there was an overall acknowledgement that British companies could expand into this fast-growing market. In a post-Brexit world, Somaliland is well positioned to unlock a new dimension in UK-African trade. Particularly through Somaliland's Berbera port - a growing trade and logistics hub that has attracted investment from Dubai's DP World.

Somaliland Somalia disconnected

My third area of reflection is on Somaliland-Somalia issues: as just noted, one thing that was soundly dismantled in the debate was the argument that recognising Somaliland would destabilise Somalia, or linked to this, that Somaliland needs to negotiate with Somalia and to convince them to agree to Somaliland's independence in order for Somaliland to win international recognition. This was convincingly rebutted. One MP called the suggestion that Somalia exercises any meaningful control of Somaliland as "frankly nonsense". Mr Clive Betts from Sheffield South East dismissed the idea that "Mogadishu now has any remit in Somaliland" as "a piece of nonsense, and it is time the [UK] Government recognised that."

But the most resounding refutation came from Hon Rushanara Ali, who drew a parallel between the case of

Somaliland-Somalia and that of Bangladesh-Pakistan. She recalled the fact that the UK Government "took a leadership role and supported the right to self-determination of the country in which I[she] was born [Bangladesh] during the war of independence between Pakistan and Bangladesh." Hon Ali reminded those present that the UK Government "did not say that Pakistan should determine the future of the independence of what became Bangladesh" and dismissed the idea that such a principle should be applied in the case of Somaliland as ridiculous.

Recognising the sovereignty, independence and achievements of Somaliland instead would be a key step to enabling Somalia itself to realise the internal peace which has alluded it for three decades. Specifically, it would provide a peace dividend for Somalia by allowing its Federal Government to focus on securing its own borders and stability. By recognising Somaliland independence - which is already a reality on the ground – the Federal Government could focus on improving to govern Somalia. Somalia's Federal Government frankly should not concern itself with Somaliland which has already proven itself far more capable of governing itself. Somaliland's success in that regard and its stability should not be undermined by sustained commitment to a thoroughly discredited position on federal unity. Recognising Somaliland will enhance Somalia's stability, not degrade it, while consolidating Somaliland's own impressive achievements.

Somaliland's identity as a country is unique in the context of the Somali Peninsula. The Somali Republic had only two constituent countries: Somaliland and Somalia. It was formed by the union of these two previously separate and independent states. This creates an implicit situation in which there are no legal, historical, or political bases on which regions of what was the Somali Republic could secede. A separation between the only two entities that united to form the Somali Republic is therefore only that: a dissolution of a union between the two parties rather than the secession of a single region amongst many. In other words, it would constitute the dissolution of a union between two equal states, just as in the case of Gambia and Senegal when their union was dissolved. The consensus view is that Somaliland has an exceptional and uniquely justified case for international recognition and a proven 30-year track record of governing itself: a record that obviously far exceeds that of Somalia.

Next move

The fourth and last point that needs to be considered is 'what to do now?' This debate marked an important move towards the fulfilment of the desire of Somaliland to gain nothing less than full International Recognition. But obviously there is more work needed to achieve that goal. This moment must not therefore be seen as an end, but as an important step to build upon. I am not sure, in the history of the UK Parliament, if there has been such an engaging debate on a Somaliland issue before. For the last three decades it certainly hasn't happened. I have since seen few people, obviously anti-Somaliland, who have tried to downgrade what happened yesterday! But we need to build on this momentum by:

- first recognizing that this is not an isolated accident, but it linked to the great coordinated moves that the current Somaliland Executive have made, including the excellent work done by Somaliland Representative in the USA and the recent interest of Americans in engaging more meaningfully with Somaliland through business and other relations. This led to the recent visit of the staff of the US Senate to Somaliland.
- it should be also linked to the new conversation that has recently recommenced between the Somaliland and Ethiopian governments, including with the visit of the Somaliland Presidential delegation to Addis Ababa, which sends another important signal.
- prior to this, Somaliland opened its doors for Taiwan as a gateway to Africa, a successful foreign relation between the two countries, from which resident Amb. Allen Chenhwa Lou broadly affirms that in Hargeysa, he represents "Taiwan in 10 East African countries", and that Somaliland makes debut at Taipei International Food Show. China may see this relationship as an unnerving element in its policy in Africa, but Somaliland government managed wisely and firmly the conversation.
- with those acknowledgements, we now need to call for all Somalilanders in the diaspora in other

countries to take similar steps to work in their own countries while the mood is ripe for further advances such as those achieved in the US and the UK.

- finally, despite the 'formal answer' from the FCDO to the debate, the UK Government is convinced the chances for Somaliland to improve, and both the recent updates on security travel advice and supporting of the CDC Group to invest in Berbera, give a signal.

Somaliland need to capture that message and for instance insist on upgrading the UK Office in Hargeysa to full diplomatic mission. In conclusion, I think there was a fundamental factor that really made a difference in the UK: those MPs who have visited Somaliland had a much stronger voice as a result of their experience and thus being able to speak out convincingly on things that they knew from personal experience. Gavin Williamson, Stephen Doughty, Clive Betts and others who had visited Somaliland were prominent in the debate and in pressing Somaliland's case. This is a significant factor and underlines the importance of engaging with politicians in countries such as the UK. As we used to say, *"i tus oo i taabsii"*, show me with facts. Somaliland showed them with facts that it is a credible partner, reliable for mutual investment, fostering democratic values, and as a partner for a better world for tomorrow. Somaliland has been a stable, peaceful, democratic country in the Horn of Africa for 30 years. It has democratically elected successive governments with relatively effective and developing institutions, with seven peaceful transitions of power- an achievement that sets it miles apart from many countries on the continent. Somaliland has shown itself to be a responsible and mature member of the international community and has good relations with neighbouring countries in East Africa. Somaliland also co-operates comprehensively with the International Community on counter terrorism, antipiracy and maritime security. Somaliland for the past 30 years has therefore been an anchor for stability. It plays a key role in securing its 850km Gulf of Aden coastline, including key maritime routes critical to African and global trade. This is critical to international logistics and supply chains. This has been much to the benefit of Africa and indeed the rest of the world.

Recognising Somaliland now would cement this anchor of peace, stability, and security in a strategically important region. This message that we have been repeating so loudly for thirty years, has been now said by others with a more powerful microphone than us, Somalilanders.

The day after
Somalilanders at home and in the Diaspora have been celebrating since the debate. Popular and lively celebration and debates in social media have been highly visible since then. The Somaliland Parliament endorsed a motion by MP Mohamed Hussein from Hargeysa, to formally thank the UK MPs on behalf of Somaliland.

Opposition leaders expressed with words of appreciation the initiative. Thursday's cabinet meeting, chaired by the President approved a similar endorsement while community-led, government backed, public demonstrations, expressing support for the debate, thanking the initiator, the Rt Hon Gavin Williamson, and other MPs, have been colourfully ongoing in all major cities of the Republic of Somaliland.

Unedited Keynote speeches

In this chapter I report unedited keynote speeches of the President and other keynote speakers who spoke on public events. I do not publish the discussion and talk points of the meetings that were not public. To report the outcome from these meetings, I used the personal reflections in the first chapter and in the introduction, as well as the reactions from the delegate members on specific issues within those meetings. When found interestingly contributing comments, publicly said by any member of the delegates in a formal answer, I equally reported in chapter one. In this chapter therefore you will find presidential speeches at the Heritage Foundation, George Washington University, Washington Institute for Near East Policy, Presidential dinner with Somaliland Community in North America. We also included the speech of Minister Shukri H Ismail Mahmoud "Bandare", the minister for Environment and Climate Change for the launch event at International Conservation Caucus Foundation (ICCF), and the plenary speech of Dr Kevin Roberts, Director of Heritage Institute.

President Muse Bihi: The Heritage Foundation

Remarks By President Muse Bihi Abdi at The Heritage Foundation
March 14, 2022

I. Introduction

Good afternoon, I would like to extend my sincere gratitude and appreciation to Dr. Kevin Roberts, President of the Heritage Foundation, for inviting me to give this address today.

The Heritage Foundation stands out among America's leading public policy institutions for promoting a truly interdisciplinary approach to understanding the politics and economics of East Africa. It is therefore a great pleasure and an honor for me to exchange views today on Somaliland and the future of our region with such distinguished participants.

Ladies and Gentlemen

Today the whole world is laser-focused on the tragedy in Ukraine. The shelling, the bombardment, the destruction, the death, the mass suffering, and the largest refugee crisis in Europe. Today, the suffering of the people of Ukraine is unfolding in front of our own eyes with the help of the 24/7 news cycle and social media. For us, this tragedy is reminiscent of the genocide committed against our people 33 years ago.

A tragedy I myself witnessed firsthand and which over 50,000 of our people were massacred at the hands of the Somalia government and more than a million of our people became either refugees or were internally displaced. We feel the pain and the anguish that the people of Ukraine feel today because we went through the same experience. Only in our case, the genocide committed against our people was hidden from the world as at that time there were no 24/7 news cycles or social media. However, the bitter memory of what we went through is forever memorized in our minds and will never be forgotten.

Ladies and gentlemen: I come before you today to talk about my country's progress, challenges, and the role my country plays in the security, stability, and economic development in our region and beyond.

II. Somaliland's journey toward independence

Somaliland first gained independence and international recognition on 26 June 1960. Five days after independence, Somaliland united voluntarily with Somalia with the aim of creating a "Greater Somalia" comprised of five former colonies inhabited by citizens of ethnic Somali origin (British Somaliland, Italian Somaliland, French Somaliland, the current Somali Region of Ethiopia, and the then Northern Frontier District of Kenya). Unfortunately, this union, which was never legally formalized, became more bane than boon.

The dream of a greater Somalia not only did not materialize but caused untold suffering and devastation for the Somali ethnic group and the broader Horn of Africa region.

The hastily arranged union became untenable for Somaliland as our people were subjected to increasing autocratic rule and oppression from Mogadishu. Initially, the civilian government of the Somali Republic through administrative takeover reduced Somaliland to the status of junior partner in the union. This power grab and deliberate domination did not go down well with our people, and they start to resist Somalia's design of domination.

Early dissatisfaction with the union-led the majority of Somaliland voters to reject the unitary constitution in a June 1961 referendum, and in December of that year Somaliland officers launched an unsuccessful coup in Hargeysa, with the aim of restoring Somaliland's independence.

The military regime that seized power in October 1969 continued systematic discrimination against the people of Somaliland. The formation of the Somali National Movement (SNM) in 1981 was a manifestation of the discontent of the people of Somaliland. Any attempt by the people of Somaliland to seek their lawful rights was met with extreme brutality, extra-judicial executions, disappearances, arbitrary arrests, detention, and torture.

In May 1988, the SNM launched successful assaults against Hargeysa and Burao. The conflict erupted into a full-scale civil war. The military regime answered with indiscriminate bombardment and deliberate targeting of the civilian population. Hargeysa, the Somaliland capital was razed to the ground. Other cities were also systemically targeted and destroyed. The regime's genocidal actions were in effect an act of ethnic cleansing. Evidence of widespread war crimes committed against the people of Somaliland has been fully documented by the United Nations Special Rapporteur for Human Rights and a forensic team from Physicians for Human Rights, as well as the Somaliland War Crimes Commission.

After the collapse of the Somali state in 1991, the people of Somaliland decided to withdraw from the union and re-assert Somaliland's sovereignty and independence – in full compliance with international law and the charter of the African Union. To fully understand the Somaliland people's desire for independence, all we need is to look at the tragic history of oppression, human rights violation, and genocide experienced by the people of Somaliland at the hands of the Somalia government.

In the three decades that followed, the people of Somaliland built a functioning state, a successful market economy, and a vibrant democracy.

Inclusive and transparent elections have been a critical element in the consolidation of the Somaliland state and its validation by our people.

These elections, which in recent years have been among the first to use advanced iris biometric verification technology, are widely endorsed by international observers as free and fair and have led to repeated peaceful and orderly transfers of power. These include Somaliland's combined parliamentary and local councils elections last May, held in the midst of the COVID-19 pandemic. We look forward to continuing this tradition with more elections later this year.

My country, Somaliland, is often celebrated for its functioning, stable and democratic state in an otherwise volatile region. We do not wish to be extraordinary. But similarly sustained democratic progress in our part of the world is rare.

We have deterred terrorists from our land and pirates from our coastal waters.

Somaliland is rightfully very proud of the security, stability, and democracy we enjoy, and I am pleased to say we celebrated 30 years of independence in May of last year. Somaliland has now been outside the union with Somalia more than we have been inside the union.

We are confident that, in time, the world will come to acknowledge what an African Union fact-finding mission to Somaliland concluded in 2005 – that Somaliland's search for recognition is "historically unique and self-justified." And our ultimate goal remains: to gain international recognition as an independent nation and assume our rightful place within the international community. Yet while we maintain this aspiration, in the short-term the focus of our diplomacy is a deeper engagement with those who share our values – especially the United States. This pragmatic and patient approach has helped Somaliland emerge in recent years as a reliable partner in a critical region.

III. Somaliland's geopolitical significance and shared interests with like-minded countries.

First, the security situation in Somalia has deteriorated dramatically, provoking a reevaluation of the political considerations that impeded more direct engagement between the U.S. and Somaliland.

As you will recall, the U.S. re-established diplomatic ties with Somalia in 2013, guided by a vision of an empowered central government in Mogadishu that could build domestic unity among disparate clans, degrade and defeat extremism and protect its people and its neighbors from the scourge of terrorism and instability.

That vision was not realized.

Today, even those most committed to empowering the Mogadishu government have lost faith in the project. Time and time again, Mogadishu's partners have expended financial resources, diplomatic resources, and military resources, with little to show for the effort.

Regrettably, after nearly a decade of good intentions by Mogadishu's partners and considerable U.S. and international assistance, the Somalia government lacks legitimacy and struggles to exercise its authority beyond Mogadishu. It remains a source of instability in our fragile region.

The second major development is that the Horn of Africa has become a region of heightened strategic importance. In a difficult neighborhood, Somaliland's stability and reliability are increasingly recognized as an asset for advancing the interests of countries who share the same values.

In recent years, the stability of the Horn of Africa has also been challenged by conflicts in the region, as well as the constantly evolving operations of terrorist groups. Instability and food insecurity is further exacerbated by drought, desertification, locust swarms, and climate change effects.

Simultaneously, the Bab el-Mandeb Strait has emerged as a vital strategic link in maritime trade routes connecting the Atlantic Ocean and the Mediterranean

Sea to the Indian Ocean. A significant portion of the world's oil passes through Bab el-Mandeb, as well as considerable trade between Europe and Asia. Its importance is reflected in the expansion of foreign military bases and buildup of naval forces in the Red Sea, as well as enhanced international cooperation to fight piracy and ensure maritime security.

Great power competition in Africa will continue for the foreseeable future. In this environment, the United States should make clear its support for governments that embrace democratic governance and stability in the midst of threats, instability, and external pressure.

IV. The Third major development is Somaliland's emergence as a trade and shipping hub.

The modernization of the Port of Berbera, the opening of a new international airport, and the construction of commercial corridors to inland neighbors are connecting the Horn of Africa to global trade routes, serving as a linchpin for renewed economic development in East Africa.

Last June, our government and DP World inaugurated a new container terminal at the Berbera Port, marking the completion of the first phase of a significant port expansion project. This was followed in October with DP World and Britain's development finance agency announcing plans to jointly invest a significant amount of money in logistics infrastructure in Africa, starting with the further modernization of Berbera Port.

These investments, combined with ongoing challenges in neighboring countries, make Somaliland the most stable and reliable conduit between much of East Africa and the world's major shipping lanes.

Taken together, these three developments – the challenges the international community confronts in the Horn of Africa, its increasingly strategic importance, and Berbera's potential to create a new economic engine for the region – mean that Somaliland is poised to become a key player in global security and economy.

Somaliland/Somalia Dialogue
The Somaliland/Somalia dialogue started with the London Conference of 23 February 2012. Article 6 of the London conference stated that" "the conference recognized the need for the international community to support any dialogue that Somaliland and TFG (Transitional Federal government) or its replacement may agree to establish to clarify their future relations."

The key point here is to clarify the future relations between the two countries. Therefore, in order to clarify the future relations between the two countries, the core issues of the dispute, namely the status of Somaliland, would have to be addressed and resolved.

Despite nine rounds of talks between 2012 and 2022, the expected outcome of the talks, resolving the core issues of the dispute, the status of Somaliland, never materialized as there was no political breakthrough. The limited agreements made on the peripheral technical issues were never implemented as Somalia reneged on all of the agreements made. During those ten years, Somalia has demonstrated a complete lack of interest in meaningful dialogue. In fact, Somalia has used the dialogue to pursue policies aimed at weakening Somaliland's independence and its ability to develop including weaponizing international aid and economic development.

Given that there has been no progress over the last ten years since the dialogue between Somaliland and Somalia started, Somaliland believes that the dialogue had failed to achieve its objective. The reasons for the failure lie entirely with Somalia's efforts to undermine the dialogue process as demonstrated by its harmful actions, willful disregard of the agreements made, and its intransigencies.

Given that dialogue is not an option for Somalia as demonstrated by its conduct, bad faith, and continuous sabotage of the dialogue, Somaliland believes that it is unfair to Somaliland to be beholden to a dialogue process that has failed to achieve its objective and has no hope of succeeding. It is difficult to imagine that what has not been achieved in 10 years can be achieved in one or two years.

Somaliland, therefore, believes that there is no future in the continuation of dialogue with Somalia and is prepared to pursue all available avenues for international recognition.

Given above, Somaliland believes that the international community has a moral obligation to support Somaliland's pursuit of international recognition.

V. The merits and promise of closer US-Somaliland collaboration

In fact, this chapter has already begun. From regional security to democracy promotion to economic development, the objectives, and values sought by the United States align entirely with Somaliland's vision.

Recent months have seen an increase in engagement and collaboration, including productive visits by the Somaliland Foreign Minister to Washington, and the recent visit to Hargeysa by a delegation of senior U.S. congressional staff – a historic first for Somaliland.

I am very heartened by these developments. But sustained direct dialogue and partnership is needed if we are to effectively address the growing challenges and truly advance our shared security, economic, and governance objectives in the region.

An important foundational element of this partnership is the establishment of a permanent U.S. diplomatic presence in Hargeysa. Several nations – including Ethiopia, the United Kingdom, Denmark, Kenya, Taiwan, Turkey, and the UAE – have diplomatic offices in our capital, and the United States should join their ranks. With this presence and regular visits by senior U.S. officials, we will be able to cooperate more closely in a number of key areas.

Let me briefly highlight a few areas where Somaliland's capabilities and proven track record can be a valuable resource for like-minded countries.

As I noted earlier, Somaliland has successfully deterred threats to our homeland and piracy in our territorial waters. Our Coast Guard works with partners such as the UK to guarantee the safety and security of maritime trade through the Red Sea and the Gulf of Aden, and we work with foreign partners and international NGOs to minimize illicit trafficking and smuggling networks. We have much to offer in terms of community-based security successes, and closer collaboration with the U.S. on these efforts would advance shared interests and strengthen its needed presence in the region.

Similarly, our recently modernized infrastructure, particularly the Port of Berbera, is well-positioned to support security operations, logistics, and humanitarian aid, as well as expand commercial opportunities throughout the region. We appreciate the U.S. government's interest in Berbera and hope discussions will continue to explore utilization and further development of what could be a vital gateway for trade, investment, and security collaboration.

On governance issues, Somaliland's democratic government is the only one of its kind in the region. It serves as a beacon for our neighbors and others whose citizens seek opportunities to engage in the democratic process. Over the last 30 years, we have built our democratic norms and institutions and ensured more than three peaceful transitions of power.

We are aware that there are still certain issues to be addressed to ensure that our electoral process is more perfect. We are working on ways and means, within our laws, of enhancing the role of women in our political process and increasing their participation, as candidates, in future elections.

Somaliland has much to offer others seeking to build their own democratization processes. From updating voter registration systems to ensuring the objectivity of national election authorities, and from managing polling stations to facilitating the work of independent election monitors, we have 20 years of practical experience to share. We would welcome greater partnership with the U.S government and civil society organizations to advance democratic norms in our region and elsewhere – and to further improve our own institutions.

VI. Conclusion

In a troubled region that has experienced significant setbacks for democratic governance and continues to face serious threats from terrorists and other violent extremist groups, the successes of Somaliland are no small achievement. Our friends in the United States understand this, and we are grateful for their continued engagement and support.

Yet this is just the beginning. We can and must work more closely together if we hope to compete with – and overtake – those who seek further instability and dependency in our region.

There are so many practical and important steps we can take. And with each one, Somaliland will demonstrate to our partners and the world that our ultimate goal of international recognition should be granted.

As an equal with other nations, Somaliland will be able to contribute even more effectively to a sustainable and prosperous future for the Horn of Africa, building on our own experience in forging an oasis of stability in a long-troubled region.

The road ahead may be long but I am more confident than ever that Somaliland will be able to count on U.S.

support as we pursue shared objectives and journey toward our long-deferred destination: a free, sovereign, and democratic Somaliland.

Thank you

President Muse Bihi: George Washington University

Remarks by President Muse Bihi Abdi at
George Washington University - March 22, 2022

Good afternoon, I would like to extend my appreciation to the George Washington University, the Elliott School of International Affairs, and Jennifer Cooke, the Director of the Institute for African Studies, for inviting me to give this address today. As a top research university in the nation's capital, the George Washington University is educating the next generation of American leaders. It is therefore a great pleasure and an honor for me to speak to you all about Somaliland and the future of our region.

I am also happy to be speaking at a university named after a great leader in America's effort to gain independence and recognition from the international community. Somaliland today also enjoys independence but continues to work toward recognition that was vital to America's success as a young nation.

Somaliland is former British Protectorate with international borders. United with Somalia on free will and left Somalia on free will following genocide where we lost about 100,000 people. Its population is roughly 4.5 million, and the physical area of the country is 176,200 Sq. Km. Somaliland is a democratic, multi-political parties, run by presidential governance with two chamber parliamentary system, namely House of representatives, house of elders. Since 2022 there have been six elections, freely contested with one person one vote.

Somaliland fulfils all the requirements of a sovereign state. It is a peaceful, stable and has a strong active force which is also the guardian of the Red Sea for safe passage for one third of the economy of the world. So far, Somaliland rebuilt cities, rebuilt educational system — over 1,000 schools, developed higher education with universities in all regions, and rebuilt health services with over 400 health care centres in the country.

Somaliland economics is based on liberal free market with GDP of $3billion in 2020, and international trade of $1.6 billion (2020). Somaliland created an ecosystem that facilitated and attracted international investors like DP World, ADDF, Coca Cola, Genel Energy, CPC (Taiwan) and others. The main source for financing public services is from domestic taxes. No budgetary support, no budget deficit, and most importantly no external debt.

On International Relations, Somaliland has representatives in 28 countries, while Hargeysa counts consulates from Djibouti, Ethiopia, Kenya, UAE, Turkey, Taiwan with offices from Denmark and UK. Somaliland wants peaceful co-existence Somaliland and has strong vision of regional economic integration.

Somaliland welcomes USA engagement, and wants to collaborate with USA on areas like, security (i.e., intelligence, coast guard, training); investment in natural resources (i.e., minerals and oil); contribution to the development of Berbera — Addis Ababa Corridor; elections to support the delivery of one-person-one-vote democratic free and fair elections; direct aid via USAID and other USA channels. Somaliland proposes a physical USA representation in Hargeysa — consulate, and when it comes to this engagement, Somaliland requires to reinstate a two-state dual track policy which distinguishes Somaliland from Somalia. Somaliland asks USA to give the same support that has been given to South Sudan.

President Muse Bihi: Washington Institute for Near East Policy

Remarks by President Muse Bihi Abdi
The Washington Institute for Near East Policy, March 22, 2022

Good afternoon.

I would like to extend my sincere gratitude to the Washington Institute for Near Institute and Policy and Executive Director Robert Satloff for inviting me to exchange views today on Somaliland and the future of the Red Sea region. I also want to thank David Schenker for leading this important discussion, and all of you for participating.

I am joined today by several members of my cabinet, including Foreign Minister Dr. Essa Kayd, as well as our Representative to the U.S., Bashir Goth, and senior advisors. My delegation has come to Washington to meet with officials in the Biden Administration, Congress, Senate, and institutions like yours to convey one simple message: our ultimate goal is international recognition, but as a first step we seek strong engagement and partnership with the United States.

I look forward to hearing your perspectives on recent developments in the Horn of Africa through a Middle East lens following a few introductory remarks. Let me begin with some history. Somaliland first gained independence and international recognition on 26 June 1960. Five days after independence, Somaliland united voluntarily with

Somalia, which had just become liberated from Italian colonial rule. Our aim was to create a "Greater Somalia" comprised of five former colonies inhabited by citizens of ethnic Somali origin.

Unfortunately, this union, which was never legally formalized, became untenable for Somaliland. Our people were subjected to autocratic rule, oppression and eventually war by Mogadishu. As the Somali state collapsed in 1991, our people re-claimed Somaliland's sovereignty and independence — in full compliance with international law and the charter of the African Union. And in the three decades that followed, the people of Somaliland have built a functioning state, a successful market economy and a vibrant democracy.

With little international assistance, the Government of Somaliland has successfully kept our territory free from piracy, minimized illicit trafficking and smuggling networks, and worked alongside partners to guarantee the safety and security of maritime trade through the Red Sea and the Gulf of Aden. We advance these common objectives with being recognized as partners.

As the geopolitical environment in the Middle East and East Africa continues to evolve, Somaliland's contributions to maritime security and trade in this critical region are more important than ever before. Many regional players — particularly those in the Middle East, like the United Arab Emirates, Turkey, Qatar and Iran — and global powers like Russia and China, have increasingly recognized the strategic importance of having a role and presence in the Red Sea.

As foreign military bases expand, and naval forces increasingly patrol in the Horn of Africa, countries that border the Red Sea and the Gulf of Aden are increasingly acting upon our common security challenges. Similarly, we are pursuing shared economic opportunities as new infrastructure and trade flows re-shape markets.

In many ways, the arbitrary division of the Middle East, the Indo-Pacific region and the Horn of Africa has been short-sighted. Our countries have shared political, economic and cultural ties for decades, if not centuries. For example, the export of livestock to the Arabian Peninsula has long been a cornerstone of Somaliland's economy.

The Red Sea is one of the world's most vital global trade routes, through which a significant percentage of global shipping passes annually. A large portion of the world's oil passes through Bab el-Mandeb, as well as considerable trade between Europe and Asia. Somaliland, like all countries that share these waters, depends on the Red Sea for trade and transit. It is therefore only natural that a more comprehensive regional architecture would emerge to manage the challenges we share. We are encouraged that this is now happening.

Policy experts and policy makers who focus on the Middle East and East Africa are coming together to address these matters. Somaliland has more than 460 miles of coastline along the Gulf of Aden's entrance to the Red Sea, and has much to contribute to the diplomatic dialogue among states that border this strategic maritime region. Our lack of international recognition should not be a reason for our exclusion from these efforts.

As a more integrated diplomatic dialogue takes shape, economic integration is also accelerating — with Somaliland playing a critical role as an emerging trade and shipping hub. Last June, our government and Dubai-based ports operator DP World opened a new container terminal at the Port of Berbera. This marked the completion of the first phase of a significant port expansion and modernization project. In October, DP World and Britain's development finance agency announcing plans to jointly invest in new infrastructure in East Africa, including the construction of commercial corridors to Ethiopia and other inland neighbors. Thanks to the modernization of the Port of Berbera, the opening of a new international airport, and other new investments in key sectors of our economy, Somaliland has become the most stable and reliable conduit between much of East Africa and the world's major shipping lanes.

As I noted at the beginning of my remarks, I came to Washington to seek meaningful engagement and partnership with the United States. Simultaneously, we all have witnessed the deterioration of the political and security situation in Somalia. After nearly a decade of good intentions by Mogadishu's partners and much U.S. and international assistance, Somalia's government lacks legitimacy and lacks authority beyond Mogadishu. It remains a source of instability in our fragile region.

This failure is provoking a new evaluation of policies that previously impeded more direct engagement between the U.S. and Somaliland. We heard this first-hand over the course of the past week. In my meetings and consultations with U.S. Government officials, I was encouraged by their interest in closer relations with Somaliland. The Biden Administration has agreed to deepen cooperation on key shared objectives, including maritime security, counterterrorism, humanitarian assistance, environmental protection, and business promotion. Much of this will directly involve our role in the Red Sea.

Our delegation received an equally warm welcome in Congress, where Somaliland today has more friends than at any point in our history. Last week, a bipartisan group of Senators introduced the "Somaliland Partnership Act", and similar actions were taken in the House of Representatives.

These bills would require the Defense and State Departments to study the feasibility of a security partnership between the U.S. and Somaliland. This truly signals a new chapter in our relations with the United States.

Our friends here understand that in a troubled region that continues to face instability, poor governance and threats from terrorists, the successes of Somaliland are no small achievement. We are grateful for their continued engagement and support.

From regional security and intelligence cooperation to democracy promotion and economic development, the objectives and values sought by the United States align entirely with Somaliland's vision for the Horn of Africa.

I look forward to discussing how, together, we can advance these shared priorities.

Thank you.

President Muse Bihi: Somaliland Community Event

I would like to thank all the organizers and the participants of this information-sharing meeting, I know some of you traveled from Canada and across North America, and I sincerely thank you for that on behalf of the members of this delegation. We are sorry that the meeting hall was not enough for all of us and someone of you are outside during this cold weather, I am so grateful for your sacrifices and your time, I sincerely again thank you. I would like to thank and welcome the head of the Somaliland Mission in the USA, Bashir Sh. Omar who did an amazing job, he is a historic man, who organized this trip for the delegation to come here and let the world know our story. We would like to hear your views as well on this trip we consider successful.

To Somaliland Diaspora all over the world and especially in North America, your fathers and your grandfathers were the heroes that brought the Somali independence and the freedom fighters. There were around ten men who were seaman at that time, who use to live in the coastline areas of America, like New York, Baltimore, and cities like. When the Second World War started in the 1940s and the whole of Africa wanted to get their freedom. People who went to the United Nations and represent the Somali case, with the request of not diving the Somali people (In all five Somali nations), were Somali diaspora in South America and they have pages in Somali history.

At the beginning of SNM, that movement started in Mogadishu, Jeddah, Europe, and across the world, yet when we needed to let the world what is going on in Somaliland, the Somaliland intellectuals and educated people were the ones that updated and the United Nations and American government for the situation in Somali region; fighting against injustice and protecting against Ali Samatar and Siyad were the Somali American Youth, and that protect use to happen in here Washington. When the SNM movement started you contributed financially, to the rebuilding of telecommunication you were the first people who started, it was Dr Bulhan the first man who invested in telecommunication, the Second person was Abdikarim Mohamed Eid who was from London and started TELESOM. The people who rebuild this country in every sector, hospital, school, and university were the Somaliland diaspora, Today I won't tell you where Somaliland is going because you already knew that.

The ministers have updated you on the current situation of the country, if I try to summaries for the last eleven years the Kulmiye Party was ruling the country, that eleven years the majority of the country has been at peace, and we have been pushing Somaliland enemies to the borders, in terms of development there are three main areas, A lot of you have more experience and education then I am, however, because you have elected me to be your president I will summarize the philosophy of Somaliland for the last eleven years, *There was a man who had many arrows and they asked him which one did we remove you he said the one in my back so that I will be able to sit down.*

If you have land, you can do anything, the first thing that we have is the peace, we have been building it for the last eleven years, the second thing is health and education and they are twins, The third one is the water, Somaliland is suffering lack of water, for the last eleven years, Kulmiye has been building our national army. The fact if for the last eleven years Somaliland army has increased 100% in terms of quality, education, and number.

Coming to the water we have dug more than two hundred fifty water wells, and most of the are located in the eastern parts of Somaliland, water wells are not enough for the local community, causing the community over the number the water wells, plus the water wells need sustainability and educated engineers to work on it is maintenance, and mainly they work only two years and with the expenditure of $200,000, for that reason we start building water dams for the coming five years, invested by the World bank.

The world bank said that we will send money through Somalia, and we said that we don't need from coming from Somalia, Dr. Osman and Dr. Saad Ali Shire have been fighting for that money, for the last years and other people helped them and that money finally reaches Somaliland it is 14 million dollars and we plan 7 million of that should go to water dams across Somaliland regions. We will start that in the dry regions, all six regions of Somaliland only Burco and Ceerigaabo have sufficient water. Starting from Boorama, there is no deep water, the closest deep water that Boorama has is in Baki, and Baki is under a mountain so it would need 300 meters to g up and then reach Boomara, which would be cost,

Gabiley is the same, Hargeysa is same, the water in Geed-deeble are or even enough a quarter of the city, and there are fourteen water wells, the whole city drinks water tank. Hargeysa needs water reserves and we have to manage our rainwater, to manage water scarcity. In Oodweyne we dug 6 water wells one of the costs us 500,000 dollars, water wells cannot feed 600 camels, Ceel-xume is one of these water wells. Our nomadic people believe that we make water dams that would damage the environment and the grass level will go down, yet that is not the fact and we will build water dam in Oodweyene, someplace near Daad-madheedh dry river, other than that the city won't be a city.

In Caynaba, Saraar region they have two problems one it is water a bitter, the second one is there is a huge distance among the water wells, it is grassland, Luckily for the last days the ten water wells that were dug in Caynabo, the first one is drinkable water and it is strong, that is good news, In the Haw of Burco before the people use to use during the drought their water wells, water reserves "Barkado" This year one of the main causes of the drought was in all Hawd region there was lack of rain from the last three years and personal water reverses were being used. From the Somali Ethiopian region, camels come to Burco for water and that was what makes the drought more severe. Consequently, we start donating water, 13 thousand water tanks have been donated, In December last year we send a letter to the international community saying there is a drought alarm in Somaliland, we asked these people who claim that they help the people these 13 thousand water tanks only 500 were from the international community, the rest of that Somaliland local community, government, businesspeople and diaspora donated. it is not all Somaliland business community people who donated are not more than five or six.

Whenever I go country or met with an international community I said "We have money and we are not begging you" Somaliland economist said that the Somaliland business community made a profit of around 2 billion dollars, and it is the reality that the Somaliland business community own more than ten billion, they have so many different savings. If they unite, they can do something big, and the main reason we are here is asking these united nations to remove sanctions from us and let our business community interact with international banks we don't want to beg you we want to develop our country, that was our message to the USA. Tonight all four big companies of Somaliland are with me and they are here TELESOM, DAHABSHIIL, Mohamed Aw-Siciid, and Omaar company, Our main goal was that our community are small in number and we all know how to do business, and we have money, so we said to America, you control the dollar which so global currency and we have Dollar, we buy the dollar in tea so, let the recognition be in another time, but what we need is didn't you recognize your money! we want the USA government to remove sanctions from us and let us interact with the international banks, we have the system and regulations. Our main goal is to reach the recognition of Somaliland businesses and banks before the political recognition and if we reach this, we would be able to solve many problems.

For the last years, particularly during my time as president's first two years, there were some security issues, it did not conflict between the Government and the civilians, it was conflict among the community, and the wars that happened thirty years ago still had an impact within the community, because people are still traumatized and it is hard to trust each other till today, I want the Islamic scholars, educators, government officials, clan leaders and everyone to work how to cure that trauma among the Somaliland community. First two years of my presidency there were fights among the Somaliland community and we lost hundreds of people in Sool, Cell-always, plus conflict resolution is costly first two years we spent above 14 million dollars in resolving these issues. For the last two years, the eastern region is stable and it is something to be grateful for ALLAH. Somaliland today there is wide peace and stability, that is my update from the country.

In this delegation, a lot of people want to know what we have met, it is the frit time that government and business community delegation visit a country the reason is we know what they want to hear and their interest is economy and money, that's is why we bring our wealth community, if *you are going to war you better have an army and it is about entertainment then you need our peats, singers, and entertainers, if you want to farms, then you need the farmers.* We want our business community to learn from America, mainly American politicians met with people who are begging them, what we are saying is take out all your humanitarian organization in our country only remove us from sanctions, we are a self-sufficient country. We are two groups of businesspeople and the economists like Sheik Osman, they had around six meetings with the world bank, other banks, and many other financial-related institutions. our people take a lesson from Americans, and Americans were eager to listen to our story, they said that never happen, people who said this is the money that we have, and we are willing to invest our people, we don't need humanitarian aid, just remove sanctions from us and we will work together, we will share with you their meetings and outcomes, yet we have good hope.

Today early morning they were thinking to hire lawyers, they said that it is an injustice that they don't have access to international banks, they have to be able to interact with the world bank while their offices and business are based in Hargeysa, we will hire lawyers and they have agreed to hire them. The other politicians we met at the two houses of parliament and many other conferences, I have good hope and I think Somaliland last many people, and they are the cost of freedom, there is no free cake, what we want the rest of the world is respect and to listen to our story. Of all the bad memories, I have is erased is the American government saying that we need each other what can we do together.

To those of you who use to write Harrison Journal and used to protest in Washington, I see most of you are bold today[laughing], you have to erase all those bad memories because today's the American government saying that we need each other what can we do together. That is the message that I want you to take.

During our time in the USA we have reached three things; One, to let the world know that we have been a peaceful country for the last three decades and that messages reached the Whitehouse and two houses of parliament, the second thing is the elections and democracy, we inform that those three different presidents have been elected directly by the civilians, two house of parliament, and three local government elections with the peaceful process, the third one is our strategic location, we had no idea what is in our land yet both east and west everyone is interested in our strategic location. Allah grants us wealth, development, peace, and good strategic location "Alhamdullilah ", and we have the power to manage our resources, one thing we have to minimize conflict among us were ever we have let us take the slogan of *what we share is more important than our differences, and I and the academicians to be the leaders of that, most of our academicians are diaspora and the most powerful place that diaspora can have political engagement in America and you are our representative in America, we want you to take lead.*

Thank you very much, you welcome us with your whole heart, and sincerely thank you again my advice to you is to people who work together and have the siblinghood connection

President Muse Bihi: Egal International Airport

Bismillah Al-Rahman Al Rahim, as-salāmu 'alaykum.

I am very pleased with the way you welcome us, all Somalilanders here today. and I am so proud of you all. We have very exciting news, to Somalilanders and their supporters, as this delegation visit was historical, and they would remember and for those who hate Somaliland this was a huge disappointment, and they were not happy about it. We have been straggling for many years, we have been building this country in so many years and fostering the peace and stability, and many years of building government institutions, we have been patient: today the most powerful nation on the globe, the USA, wants to work with us. You have witnessed what was happening in the United States of America and how they were eager to hear our story. If some people used to say the world is against us and we didn't have a platform, today the situation is different and we have the best opportunity and these powerful nations want to know more about our country and victory is very close. For the last dozen days, we have been in the USA, a prat from the three days we were traveling, the rest of the time we were working, and we have twenty-three meetings with different parts of the USA government, their businesspeople, universities, and one meeting with the United Nations in New York. We have also participated in an equal number of meetings with Somaliland diaspora all over North America, we were working both day and night.

This time we said to the US Government, we are not here begging you; we are not here to ask for your support, we have built our country and our people do deserve to get recognized before we are ready to do a collaborate with dignity, what we want to work with you is about security, politics, business, education, and social interaction. We are ready to collaborate in all these sectors. Today the reason we come here is to open that door, you all knew that we have met with the senate and congress and they both start working on ways that we would work with the US government. You have seen these parliament houses, ordering the ministry of foreign affairs to do work with Somaliland, without a mediator.

We have fulfilled our constitutional duty and we are here to say how to work finding recognition for this country, today all USA media and major other international outlets, are talking about Somaliland in so many languages, and we have met with the United Nations. I know that the sun is very hot, and I would summarize it because you knew most of what has happened in the USA: today we have started a new connection with the need for both the government and the civilians to work together. We are individuals, what the USA was respective was you, civilians where ever you are both local and diaspora, the way you have to rebuild this country, the way you make compromises, your collaboration, your democratic values, the way you elect leaders, the way you make conflict resolution, it is the respect you earned what makes USA government welcome us and respect us, today we are in a very good place (Alhamdulilah). The Somaliland case is well known today in every country, the next step is international recognition. We will go to every country and represent the Somaliland case, so in Somalia, you can cut the relationship between USA and Somaliland.

Thank you very much, I know it is very hot and sunny, but our promise is to improve Somaliland, stay unified, let's keep being siblings to each other, and support each other, and keep working on our recognitions. Thank you very much.

Minister Shukri H Ismail Mahmoud "Bandare" at the ICCF

Introduction

Thank you very much to the International Conservation Caucus Foundation for hosting this event, and thank you all for being part of this historic visit to the United States by President Musa Bihi Abdi and his delegation.

It is a privilege today to meet with the ICCF, your board members and donors about Somaliland's progress and the opportunities for greater partnership between the U.S. and Somaliland that lie ahead.

Let me briefly touch on the history of Somaliland, because learning about our past is essential to understanding our inspirations for the future.

Somaliland lies in the Horn of Africa, on the southern coast of the Gulf of Aden. It is bordered by Djibouti to the northwest, Ethiopia to the south and west, and Somalia to the East. It has an area of 176,120 square kilometres, with approximately 5 million people.

Somaliland gained its freedom from Great Britain in 1960 and soon afterwards formed a union with the former Italian Somalia, but after 30 years of strife, we reclaimed our sovereign status in 1991. Since then, we have built a democratic system of government, advanced economic growth, and ensured the security of our people - despite lacking recognition as a sovereign nation and our location in a difficult neighborhood.

It has been nearly ten years snice a delegation of this nature visited the United States. Since that time, the geopolitical environment in the Horn of Africa has evolved considerably, bringing Somaliland's interests and U.S. interests further and further into alignment. One of those areas of alignment is a shared recognition of this importance of conservation and environmental protection.

Somaliland's climate and unique challenges
Somaliland is blessed with a diverse ecosystem, home to many species of wildlife and vegetation, large mountain ranges, and more thank 850 kilometres of coastline with pristine beaches, coral reefs and rich marine life.

Unfortunately, Somaliland faces serious environmental and conservation challenges. We are on the frontline of climate change.

The overall climate of Somaliland is monsoonal, with the majority of rains coming from southwest monsoon. We are suffering from a prolonged drought that over the past few years has killed over 70 percent of the area's livestock, a major export and critical sector for country's economy. Today 810,000 people are in need of urgent assistance. We are coping with a serious water shortage, malnutrition, and food insecurity, which has also fuelled internal migration.

Despite facing number of challenges - including limited government resources, lack of direct aid, decentralization of environmental governance and donor funds allocated mainly to social programs - we are undeterred in our fight against climate change, which is led by my ministry.

What Somaliland is doing

Somaliland's Ministry of Environment and Climate Change was established in 1997 to protect the environment, promote climate change resilience and ensure sustainable livelihoods for our people.

The Ministry has developed a five-year strategic plan as a blueprint for action, in consultation with various stakeholders including sister government ministries, universities, UN agencies, INGOs, LNGOs and others, which I would welcome the opportunity to discuss with you today.

Already, we have accomplished many of the goals of our plan, which align with the UN's Sustainable Development Goals. We have:

- Developed regulations and strategies for environmental protection and conversation;
- Raised awareness and organized training workshops on natural resource management for rural communities;
- Conducted an impact assessment on energy sources and alternatives in Somaliland;
- Established 13 tree nurseries for reforestation in rural areas - which has helped to green major towns and reduce charcoal production from live trees;
- Established seasonal grazing reserves and soil and water conservation techniques;

- Safeguarded biodiversity of protected areas, including mangrove conversation programs and research on frankincense protection; and
- Developed environmental education programs through radio and TV programs.

Somaliland is also playing a critical role in the fight to curb cheetah smuggling in the Horn of Africa, which is a major transit route for wildlife traffickers seeking to access markets on the Arabian Peninsula.

When we began this work, Cheetah populations in the region were dwindling.

In the last several years, Somaliland has worked closely with international wildlife organizations, including the Cheetah Conservation Fund and other international partners, to save and rehabilitate these precious animals. The cheetah sanctuaries and wildlife refuge created through our partnership with CCF have played a significant role in rebuilding cheetah populations in our country.

Somaliland also works to ensure that traffickers do not exploit our territory for their criminal activities. This is a comprehensive undertaking to apprehend traffickers and confiscate smuggled cheetahs, and involves the Somaliland Police, our Coast Guard, our Ministry of Environment and Climate Change, and our court system.

Starting with the region's first cheetah smuggling conviction in 2018, law enforcement officials from

Somaliland have enhanced anti-poaching methods to protect wildlife and vigorous persecutions following arrests have ensured that smugglers are held accountable.

Conclusions

The challenges I have discussed are just some of the many areas where I believe the opportunity exists to expand and forge new partnerships. That is why our delegation is here in Washington this week - to meet with allies like all of you and leaders in the Biden Administration, Congress and in civil society. We seek a strong and enduring partnership with the United States.

There is much that we can accomplish together, from reforestation, to water harvesting and dam construction for drought mitigation, to support for pastoralists and improved services for livestock, to rangeland resource rehabilitation and the restoration of previous grazing reserves, to the promotion of alternative energy source.

So I look forward to discussing how, together, we can advance these shared priorities.

I would also like to invite all of you to visit Somaliland and to see first-hand the many opportunities we can unlock with your support.

Thank you again to the ICCF for hosting this luncheon, and to your board and donors for all that you do to support conservations and protect wildlife around the world.

Dr Kevin Roberts, Director of Heritage Institute

Good morning!

Those of you tuning in online it may not be morning where you are, hello and welcome from Washington DC.

Your excellency, welcome.

And to all of you here in person what a great day for this country for the Heritage Foundation and for the wonderful Republic of Somaliland.

Before we begin, I will be remiss if I didn't mention the people of Ukraine who as we speak are battling for freedom and for many of them their very lives may we pray that conflict ends soon with Ukraine whole and free. Our hearts and prayers are with them.

I also mention Ukraine because it is relevant to our discussion today. In case anyone has missed the last 4000 years of history or just the last couple of weeks.

I want you to know that the world is indeed a dangerous place for as much as we are blessed to have a peaceful neighbour and oceans to our east and west here in the United States, we can't ever be complicit about our security.

This is one of the reasons why it is so important for the US to develop strategic and amicable partnerships specially like with those our esteemed Somalilander guests here today.

Since I am an educator at heart, I must first walk us through some relevant history, but as I promise my new friend his Excellency President Abdi, I will be brief.

Somaliland's independence is not currently acknowledged by any country in the world including the United States. This wasn't always the case though; Somaliland was briefly independent in 1960 before joining the rest of Somalia. That union was ultimately rejected by the Somaliland people but not before it was too late, the world has decided that Somaliland was indistinguishable from Somalia no matter how Somalilanders felt.

In 1980's the rebellion against the brutal dictator in power brock out again in Somalia including in Somaliland. Somalia's armed forces devastated Somaliland during the fight, practically flattening its capital city.

It may in fact had been the only conflict in history that featured aircrafts taking off from a runway in the same city and then attacking with the bombs that was just one of the cruelties of that war.

In 1991 the dictatorship collapsed but the fighting continued throughout Somalia dragging it into the failed state status for two decades. We all probably are all familiar with the battle in Mogadishu better known in the US as the Black Hawk Down the incident, those awful events took place in 1993 during the period am describing. We might also be aware that al-Qaida affiliate Al-Shabaab began concurring southern Somalia in the 2000-s. This group which is still powerful had links to some of the men who perpetuated the 1998 bombings of the USA embassies in Kenya and Tanzania.

I am recounting all this because it highlights how remarkable Somaliland's experience has been. It was and it is the exception in the Somalis turmoil.

After 1991 it redeclared its independence and created a functioning state with its own army, passport, currency, and foreign policy and very importantly free elections.

Foreigners can walk in Hargeysa without security and ISIS and al-Qaida has no presence there. It is hard not to admire building a viable state amid such difficult circumstances. How Somalilanders have achieved all these is equally commendable.

They have a powerful clam for international sympathy after the devastation they suffered during the war. But they didn't wait for help from anyone else. If they had, they would have been waiting still today. No, they went instead about the businesses to rebuilding their country largely on their own.

The clans who were on the opposite side of the fight reconciled in the process and created one of the few examples of successful indigenous peaceful process. They committed to building something which was peaceful, democratic, and workable. This brings me back to why I think the US and Somaliland should be strong partners.

First this territory of its own accord has been stacked with the democratic system and process for three decades. It hasn't been perfect just like no democratic system is perfect. But the old saying that "character is how you behave when no one is watching", well, Somaliland has stayed faithful to democracy hardly when anyone was noticing. This is proof of genuine belief.

Second, let us envision where Somaliland sits: The Bab el-Mendeb where the shipping … that carries much of trade between Europe and Asia is about 70 miles away. Yemen, where American allies are fighting Iranian backed militias in al-Qaida is just across the Gulf of Aden.

Somaliland shares the border with Ethiopia Africa's second most populous country and in normal times with a landlocked economic dilemma. Somaliland recently renovated Berbera port has great potential for boosting the economy of Ethiopia and its neighbours in east Africa. Right next door to Somaliland is Djibouti which hosts a number of military bases including China's most prominent military footprint on the continent. To the west and also in a commanding position to the Babalemendeb is Eretria. In January Chinese Prime Minister Xi Jinping visited Eretria and announced a strategic partnership with that country. We need to be clear-eyed about the competition we are in with the Chinese communist party. The communist party of Chinese is America's most single formidable opponent and is devoted for advocating to autocracies such as …Russia by violating the peace and prosperity.

That refuse to cast out. America must meet this challenge with result. That will include close relation with Somaliland given its strategic position its pro American orientation and almost alone in Africa its been immune to Beijing's overtures and threats intrusion. In fact Somaliland has established ties with Taiwanese friends another unrecognized democracy the United States should support.

Those of you who are familiar with East Africa know that it is a tough neighbourhood. Sudanese hopeful transition democratic sabotaged by a coup. One of the leaders of which by the way was in Russian to strengthen ties with Putin's criminal regime. Ethiopia is caught in a terrible civil war that we also pray will end soon. Eretria is an international pray one of the five countries just voted against the un resolution condemning Russia invasion on Ukraine. Southern Somalia is paralyzed by the political imbalance and Al Shababa stays strong. And all this volatility, Somaliland has enjoyed relative calm providing evidence there is in fact a fertile ground for a true and sustainable partnership.

Finally, I believe you can call me crazy: that American policy is most effective when it is tailored to the reality. We will see a few games in east African foreign policy just not that account for the ground truth that Somaliland has been functionally independent for decades.

Count Heritage Foundation for always trumpeting that fact. So let us upgrade our policy. United States America Should strengthens its position in a precarious and important part of the world and it should do the justice by honouring the consistent aspirations of millions of Somalilanders to rule themselves and America should proudly be the first state to recognize Somaliland as an independent nation.

We look forward to that day.

In the meantime, it is my honour to introduce his excellency the President of Somaliland, Muse Bihi Abdi.

Appendix

Appendix 1: List of delegation members and the roles

Members of the delegation from Hargeysa

President Muse Bihi Abdi, the president of the Republic of Somaliland

Minister Dr Essa Kayd, Minister for Foreign Affairs and International Cooperation

Minister Mahamed Kahin Ahmed, Minister of Interior

Minister Suleiman Ali Kore, Minister of Information, National Guidance and Culture

Minister Shukri H Ismail Mahmoud "Bandare", Minster of Environment and Climate Change

Minister Maxamed Sacad, Minister of Commerce and Tourism

Dr Jama Musse Jama, Senior European Affairs Advisor to the President

Dr Osman Sh Ahmed, Economic Advisor to the President

Mr. Abdikarim Mohamed Eid, President TELESOM Somaliland

Mr. Ahmed Seid, CEO, SOMCABLE

Mr. Abdirashid Mahamed Duale, CEO, Dahabshiil Group

Ms. Fathia Jama Omaar, CEO, Omaar Group.

Staff of the President

Mubarak Taani, General Secretary of the President

Naasir Yuusuf Daahir, Director of the Media at Presidency

Maxamed Ismaaciil Salaan, Cameraman

Xamse Axmed Ismaaciil, Photographer

Members of the Somaliland Mission to the USA
Bashir Goth, Somaliland Resident Representative to USA
Yaasiin Maxamed Mire, Director of Counsellor Affairs
and Community Outreach.

Appendix 2: Somaliland Partnership Act, Senate, USA

Appendix 2 - S.3861 - Somaliland Partnership Act, Senate - United States of America

On 17 March 2022, during the 2nd session of the 117th Congress, the Senate Committee for Foreign Relations introduced S. 3861 - the Somaliland Partnership Act with the following text (see below). This is a bill to require the Secretary of State to submit annual reports to Congress on the assistance provided to Somaliland and to conduct a feasibility study, in coordination with the Secretary of Defense, on establishing a security partnership with Somaliland, without recognizing Somaliland as an independent state. The status of the Bill at the time of publication of this book is "introduced", and has its first discussion at the Senate on the 26 May 2022, and the process can be followed at the following address: https://www.congress.gov/bill/117th-congress/senate-bill/3861

Introduced in Senate (03/17/2022)
[Congressional Bills 117th Congress]
[From the U.S. Government Publishing Office]
[S. 3861 Introduced in Senate (IS)]

117th CONGRESS 2d Session - S. 3861

To require the Secretary of State to submit annual reports to Congress on the assistance provided to Somaliland and to conduct a feasibility study, in coordination with the

Secretary of Defense, on establishing a security partnership with Somaliland, without recognizing Somaliland as an independent state.

IN THE SENATE OF THE UNITED STATES
March 17, 2022

Mr. Risch (for himself, Mr. Van Hollen, and Mr. Rounds) introduced the following bill; which was read twice and referred to the Committee on Foreign Relations.

A BILL

To require the Secretary of State to submit annual reports to Congress on the assistance provided to Somaliland and to conduct a feasibility study, in coordination with the Secretary of Defense, on establishing a security partnership with Somaliland, without recognizing Somaliland as an independent state.

Be it enacted by the Senate and House of Representatives of the United States of America in Congress assembled,

SECTION 1. SHORT TITLE.

This Act may be cited as the ``Somaliland Partnership Act".

SEC. 2. SENSE OF CONGRESS.

It is the sense of Congress that--
- (1) a stronger relationship between the United States and Somaliland would provide numerous, mutually beneficial, strategic opportunities due to Somaliland's--

- o (A) geographic location in the Horn of Africa and next to the Gulf of Aden;
- o (B) democratic credentials, including peaceful transfers of power following elections; and
- o (C) relative stability in the Horn of Africa;

- (2) Somaliland's security situation, level of development, and other challenges differ significantly from the situation in Mogadishu and other regions of Somalia, which necessitates--
  - o (A) a different approach to engagement, assistance, and travel by personnel of the Department of State and the United States Agency for International Development; and
  - o (B) the avoidance of a ``one-size-fits-all'' policy approach to Somalia;

and

- (3) the status of Somaliland should not serve as an obstacle for deeper and meaningful cooperation that will serve the mutual interests of our two governments.

SEC. 3. DEFINED TERM.

In this Act, the term ``Somaliland'' means the territory that--

- (1) received its independence from the United Kingdom on June 26, 1960, before the creation of the Somali Republic;
- (2) has been a self-declared independent and sovereign state since 1991 that is not internationally recognized; and
- (3) exists as a semi-autonomous region of the Federal Republic of Somalia.

SEC. 4. REPORT ON FOREIGN ASSISTANCE AND OTHER ACTIVITIES IN SOMALILAND.

- (a) Defined Term. --In this section, the term ``appropriate congressional committees'' means--
  - o (1) the Committee on Foreign Relations of the Senate; and
  - o (2) the Committee on Foreign Affairs of the House of Representatives.

- (b) Report.--
  - o (1) In general.--Not later than September 30, 2022, and annually thereafter until the date that is 5 years after the date of the enactment of this Act, the Secretary of State, in consultation with the Administrator of the United States Agency for International Development, shall submit a report to the appropriate congressional committees that, with respect to the most recently concluded 12-month period--
    - ▪ (A) describes United States foreign assistance to Somaliland, including--
      - (i) the value of such assistance (in United States dollars);
      - (ii) the source from which such assistance was funded;
      - (iii) the names of the programs through which such assistance was administered;
      - (iv) the implementing partners through which such assistance was provided;
      - (v) the sponsoring bureau of the United States Government; and
      - (vi) if the assistance broadly targeted the Federal Republic of Somalia, the portion of such assistance that was--
      - o (I) explicitly intended to support Somaliland; and
      - o (II) ultimately employed in Somaliland;

- (B) details the staffing and responsibilities of the Department of State and the United States Agency for International Development supporting foreign assistance, diplomatic relations, consular services, and security initiatives in Somaliland, including the location of such personnel (duty station) and their corresponding bureau;

- (C) provides--
  - (i) a detailed account of travel to Somaliland by employees of the Department of State and the United States Agency for International Development, if any, including the position, duty station, and trip purpose for each such trip; or
  - (ii) the justification for not traveling to Somaliland if no such personnel traveled during the reporting period;

- (D) describes consular services provided by the Department of State for the residents of Somaliland;

- (E) discusses the Department of State's Travel Advisory for Somalia related to the region of Somaliland; and

  - (F) if the Travel Advisory for all or part of Somaliland is identical to the Travel Advisory for other regions of Somalia, justifies such ranking based on a security assessment of the region of Somaliland.

- (2) Form.--The report required under paragraph (1) shall be submitted in unclassified form, but may contain a classified annex.

SEC. 5. FEASIBILITY STUDY ON IMPROVED DIPLOMATIC RELATIONS AND A SECURITY AND DEFENSE PARTNERSHIP WITH SOMALILAND.

- (a) Defined Term.--In this section, the term ``appropriate congressional committees'' means--
  o (1) the Committee on Foreign Relations of the Senate;
  o (2) the Committee on Armed Services of the Senate;
  o (3) the Committee on Foreign Affairs of the House of Representatives; and
  o (4) the Committee on Armed Services of the House of Representatives.
- (b) Feasibility Study.--The Secretary of State, in coordination with the Secretary of Defense, shall conduct a feasibility study regarding the establishment of a partnership between the United States and Somaliland that--
  o (1) includes coordination with Somaliland government security organs, including Somaliland's Ministry of Foreign Affairs and Ministry of Defense;
  o (2) determines opportunities for collaboration in the pursuit of United States national security interests in the Horn of Africa, the Gulf of Aden, and the broader Indo-Pacifi region;
  o (3) identifies opportunities for United States training of Somaliland security sector actors to improve their professionalization and capacity; and

- (4) assesses the prospect of establishing a nonprofit corporation, to be known as the ``American Institute of Somaliland", for the purpose of conducting and carrying out programs, transactions, and other relations with Somaliland in the City of Hargeysa on behalf of the United States Government.
- (c) Report to Congress.--Not later than 180 days after the date of the enactment of this Act, the Secretary of State, in coordination with the Secretary of Defense and the heads of other relevant Federal departments and agencies, shall submit a classified report to the appropriate congressional committees that contains the results of the feasibility study required under subsection (b), including an assessment of the extent to which--
  - (1) opportunities exist for the United States to support the training of Somaliland's security sector actors with a specific focus on counterterrorism and border and maritime security;
  - (2) Somaliland's security forces were implicated, if any, in gross violations of human rights during the 3-year period immediately preceding the date of the enactment of this Act;
  - (3) the United States has provided or discussed with government and military officials of Somaliland the provision of training to security forces, including--
    - (A) where such training has occurred;
    - (B) the extent to which Somaliland security forces have demonstrated the ability to absorb previous training; and
    - (C) the ability of Somaliland security forces to maintain and appropriately utilize such training, as applicable;

- o (4) a United States security and defense partnership with Somaliland would have a strategic impact, including by protecting the United States and allied maritime interests in the Bab-el-Mandeb Strait and at Somaliland's Port of Berbera;
- o (5) Somaliland could--
  - (A) serve as a maritime gateway in East Africa for the United States and its allies; and
  - (B) counter Iran's presence in the Gulf of Aden and China's growing regional military presence;
- o (6) a United States security and defense partnership would--
  - (A) bolster security and defense cooperation and capabilities between Somaliland and Taiwan;
  - (B) stabilize this semi-autonomous region of Somalia further as a democratic counterweight to anti-democratic forces in the greater Horn of Africa region; and
  - (C) impact the capacity of the United States to achieve policy objectives in Somalia, particularly to degrade and ultimately defeat the terrorist threat posed by Al-Shabaab, the Islamic State in Somalia (the Somalia-based Islamic State affiliate), and other terrorist groups operating in Somalia;
- o (7) the extent to which an improved diplomatic relationship with Somaliland could--
  - (A) support United States policy focused on the Red Sea corridor, the Indo-Pacific region, and the Horn of Africa;

- (B) improve cooperation on counterterrorism and intelligence sharing;
- (C) enable cooperation on counter-trafficking, including the trafficking of humans, wildlife, weapons, and illicit goods; and
- (D) support trade and development, including how Somaliland could benefit from Prosper Africa and other regional trade initiatives.
- (d) Form. -- The report required under subsection (c) shall be submitted in unclassified form, but may contain a classified annex.

SEC. 6. RULE OF CONSTRUCTION.

Nothing in this Act, including the reporting requirement under section 4 and the conduct of the feasibility study under section 5, may be construed to convey United States recognition of Somaliland as an independent state.

Appendix 3: Bipartisan letter on Increased Engagement

USA - Bipartisan letter on Increased Engagement with Somaliland

On March 14, 2022, Lead Republican Michael McCaul (R-TX), Rep. Chris Smith (R-NJ), Rep. Brian Fitzpatrick (R-PA), Rep. Tom Malinowski (D-NJ), Rep. Peter Meijer (R-MI), Rep. Guy Reschenthaler (R-PA), Rep. Kay Granger (R-TX), Rep. Young Kim (R-CA), and Rep. Steve Chabot (R-OH) signed the following letter and sent to Secretary Blinken calling for increased engagement with Somaliland. The bipartisan House members group who signed the letter, was led by McCaul and Smith.

Dear Secretary Blinken,

We write to urge the Biden Administration to consider increasing and deepening engagement with Somaliland on issues of mutual diplomatic, economic, and security interests. Somaliland's geo-strategic location on the Gulf of Aden, consistent support for democracy, cooperation on countering terrorism, piracy, and other security threats in the region, relations with Taiwan, and growing economic potential warrants that the United States explore additional opportunities to partner with Somaliland.

Recent events in the Horn of Africa have upended feeble stability in the region and further jeopardized prospects for a peaceful resolution to multiple regional and domestic issues. With civil war embroiling Ethiopia, with Eritrean involvement; return to military rule in Sudan; delayed elections and political infighting fueling increasing instability in Somalia, amidst unabated terrorist activity by Al-Shabaab; and the worst drought the region has seen in over forty years, the U.S. must rethink our current strategy of engagement to address these immense challenges and the threats posed to U.S. national security interests.

Somaliland has functioned autonomously for three decades—it maintains its own security, its own financial system, and its own trade relations. Several countries in the region, including Djibouti, Ethiopia, and Kenya, maintain diplomatic relations and trade with Somaliland, even though they don't formally recognize its independence. Some appear to have increased their engagement in the past year: Ethiopia, for example, recently upgraded its diplomatic representation by promoting its representative in Hargeysa to the rank of ambassador, and Kenya opened a Liaison Office in Somaliland last year. The United Kingdom, European Union, United Arab Emirates and Turkey also have representation in Hargeysa.

Strategic engagement with Somaliland would be a critical counterweight to China's increasing investment in the Horn of Africa. Djibouti, which has long served as the U.S.'s staging ground for U.S. military operations in the region, has become vulnerable since China operationalized their own naval base just eight miles from Camp Lemonnier in 2017. One year later, two U.S. pilots suffered injuries from Chinese-deployed lasers, underscoring the significant threat presented to U.S. operations and regional access going forward. With Djibouti's debt to China reportedly increasing to more than 70 percent of its gross domestic product (GDP), China has ample leverage to gain a further foothold in the country and could conceivably pressure Djibouti for other political and strategic advantages that further undermine U.S. military operations. It is critical that the U.S. government pursues other strategic opportunities, like access to Berbera's renovated airport and port, to safeguard our economic and security objectives in the Horn of Africa against further Chinese investment in Djibouti. Somaliland presents a democratic alternative, which has consistently resisted China's encroachment, and could ensure a continued U.S. presence on the Gulf of Aden.

Somaliland also established bilateral relations with Taiwan in September 2020 and exchanged representation shortly after. Somaliland and Taiwan have maintained close engagement, and during the COVID-19 pandemic Taiwan provided Somaliland with donated COVID-19 vaccines. The U.S. should take steps to support a deepening relationship between the Somaliland and Taiwan, as required by the Taiwan Allies International Protection and Enhancement Initiative (TAIPEI) Act of 2019, (P.L. 116–135), which calls on the U.S. government to consider additional engagement with nations that have strengthened, enhanced, or upgraded relations with Taiwan. The federal government of Somalia, meanwhile, does not maintain relations with Taiwan.

This Administration has stated that strengthening Democracy and elevating democratic partners is a top global priority. Somaliland has repeatedly demonstrated the ability to hold peaceful, credible, and competitive elections and has shown a commitment to democracy and representative government for decades. USAID has partnered with the International Republican Institute and other civil society partners to support election preparations, increased transparency and voter education and deploy election observers, in fact Somaliland's 2021 elections were the first in the world to be secured by biometric iris scans. Hargeysa has made important progress to advance democracy and effective governance and the Administration should seek to consolidate and reward this, particularly amidst further democratic backsliding elsewhere in the region.

With these political, economic, and security imperatives in mind, we urge the Administration to increase diplomatic engagement with Somaliland officials, senior leadership travel, and consider a permanent presence in Hargeysa. Increased partnership with Somaliland should be a priority and will mutually benefit U.S. and Somaliland interests. We thank you for your attention to this important matter.

###

Appendix 4: Published interviews of the delegation

Congress - S.3861 - Somaliland Partnership Act
https://www.congress.gov/bill/117th-congress/senate-bill/3861/text

Foreign Affairs Committee at the United States House of Representatives - https://gop-foreignaffairs.house.gov/press-release/mccaul-smith-lead-bipartisan-letter-on-increased-engagement-with-somaliland.

Joshua Meservey, Missing Opportunities in Somaliland
https://www.heritage.org/africa/commentary/missing-opportunities-somaliland

Julian Pecquet, Somaliland Secures more US Support.
https://www.theafricareport.com/185495/somaliland-secures-more-us-support-with-presidential-visit-to-washington.

Appendix 5: AU Fact-Finding Mission to Somaliland

RESUME
AU Fact-Finding Mission to Somaliland (30 April to 4 May 2005)

I. Introduction

An AU Fact-Finding Mission visited and stayed in Somaliland from 30 April to 4 may 2005, to see the prevailing situation (political, socio-economic, security, humanitarian and other related issues) in the country and listen to the concerns of the leadership and people of Somaliland, and duly report back the findings of the Mission to the Chairperson of the African Union Commission, with recommendations for further action. The Deputy Chairperson of the Commission, H. E. Patrick Mazimhaka, led the Mission, accompanied by Dr A. M. Kambudzi, Analyst in the Peace and Security Department; Col. Jaotody Jean de Matha, Senior Military Expert, in the same Department; Mr Patrick Tigere, Head of the Humanitarian, Refugees and Displaced Persons Division in the Department of Political Affairs and Mr Dieudonne Kombo Yaya, Senior Political Officer, in the same Department.

2. Contextually, it should be recalled that the Organization of African Unity (GAM/African Union {AU) had a longstanding invitation from Somaliland to undertake a visit to the country and view the situation on

the ground. The authorities of Somaliland have also paid successive visits to the Commission in 2003, 2004, and early 2005, seeking an Observer status for Somaliland within the AU, not only to be able to follow developments on the continent, but also to gain a platform from which the country could state its case for reclaiming its 26 June 1960 independence and the recognition of the Republic of Somaliland as a sovereign state. Given the call from Somaliland, and based on his indication to the AU Executive Council in mid-2004, to dispatch a Fact-finding Mission to Somaliland, the Chairperson of the Commission, H. E. Alpha Oumar Konare, finally dispatched the Mission as indicated above.

II. Consultations and Visits of the Mission

3. The Mission held wide ranging consultations wall the main political actors other segments of the society in Hargeysa (capital): the President of the. Republic of Somaliland, members of the Cabinet members of the Somaliland Parliament, the Presidential Envoy for the Campaign for Recognition; intellectuals businesspersons and representatives of civic organizations and women associations. The Mission, accompanied by members of the welcoming Committee of Ministers, undertook visits to Berbera seaport at the Red Sea; town of Sheikh, in the interior; town of Burao, far in the interior south and the town of Borama, in the western part of the country. The visits, well received by huge crowds of town residents

and rural folk, were the scene of intense consultations between the Mission and the respective mayors and other senior government officials, local political leaders; chiefs, elders and the representatives of civic organizations and women leaders. The Mission also visited some educational and vocational training centers. The message was the same at every place: *"the Irreversible independence of Somaliland; the irreversible sovereignty of Somaliland; no return to the Union with Somalia; the quest for recognition from the AU and the international community"*. Those visits also gave an opportunity to the Mission to witness-the legacy of the campaign of destruction by the Siyad Barre army; the destruction wrought by the civil war and its consequences on the civilian population (camps housing IDPs and Returnees, landmine fields, mass graves, disrupted physical and social infrastructures); inversely; the same visits were a window for the Mission the tremendous efforts deployed in the reconstruction of the country and the rehabilitation of the social fabric.

4. In response, the Mission undertook to convey the message and sentiments of the authorities and people of Somaliland and to report on the situation that it had witnessed in the country to the Chairperson of the Commission.

III. Overall assessment of the situation in Somaliland

5. There was an evident conviction and emotion among the Somalilanders that their "country" has all the attributes of an independent sovereign State, which they say the international community should objectively consider. At the same time, there was a rejection in lotto of the idea of re-uniting with Somalia. The famous words "No more Mogadishu; no more Somalia; Somaliland is an independent country; we want recognition; it is our right", addressed to the Fact-Finding Mission throughout its stay, visits and consultations bear testimony.

6. Since the disintegration of Somalia provoked by the collapse of the Siyad Barre administration in early 1991, leading to the breakaway of Somaliland into a self-declared independent Republic, there has been an accelerated process of state building. That process was anchored, and remains so, on the recognition by the Somalilanders of the inherited colonial borders at the time of independence from Britain in June 1960:

a. Somaliland has a constitution that emanated from grassroots consultations and was sealed in the referendum held in 2003; the constitution serves as the basic Law in Somaliland and does enjoy respect in the political practice in Somaliland. The Constitution provides for the relevant arms of government and the effective separation of powers that go along it.

b. Somaliland has territory as defined by the colonial borders inherited from the British colonial rule on accession to independence in 1960. In the north, the country is bordered by the Red Sea and the Gulf of Aden adjoining into the Indian Ocean; Puntland State borders it on the east, the while Ethiopia neighbors it on the west. To the north-west, Somaliland is bordered by Djibouti.

c. Somaliland has a population that is estimated by local sources at 3.5 million resident in the country and one million living in the Diaspora, the majority of which fled the civil
war. The Somali language is spoken throughout the country, whilst English and Arabic are also used in official and business transactions. It is not unusual to encounter those Somalis who can speak Swahili and Italian.

e. Somaliland has only declared its own independence, after "reclaiming it from the collapsed union". But the international community has not recognized that independence thus far. However, there is a standing army with a "mandate to defend the independence and territorial integrity of Somaliland".

f. Somaliland has achieved peace and stability, through a horse-grown disarmament, demobilization and re-Integration process and internally driven democratization;

g. Somaliland has a real economic potential, based on its surface and sub-surface resources and maritime resources.

IV. Findings of the Mission

7, The AU Fact-Finding Mission found out the following aspects during its three working days in Somaliland and in the different sectors:

a. Since its declaration of independence in 1991, Somaliland has been steadfastly laying the foundations of a democratic State, clothed with the relevant attributes of a "modern State". Those foundations include the Constitution of Somaliland which entrenches, among other aspects, the separation of power between the three arms of government; balance of political forces built upon the functional co-habitation of traditional governance institutions, as embodied in the political role of the clan elders and elected representatives; the existence of active opposition political parties with some capacity to influence public policy and a budding independent press;

b. The plethora of problems confronting Somaliland in the political, socio-economic, military, humanitarian and other sectors stem from two main factors, namely, the legacy of a political union with Somalia, which malfunctioned, brought destruction and ruin, thereby overburdening the population; the lack of recognition of Somaliland as an "independent sovereign State" by the international community to enable it undertake international, political, social, economic and other relevant functions and transactions and the significant, and yet untapped economic potential.

c. Somaliland and Somalia entered into a "Union" in July 1960, based on a shared ambition among the Somalis to build a "Greater Somalia", which was to incorporate all the Somali communities in the Horn of Africa. In the course of time, the Union malfunctioned. The legacy of the abortive union and the resulting civil war left behind a trail of physical destruction and social dislocation, all of which require more resources in order for the population to recover and enjoy better conditions of life.

e. Though credit has to be given to Somaliland for promoting a democratic order, and within a shorter span of time, there are gaps that need attention from both the policy makers and the individual citizens. One critical gap lies in gender relations in terms of the predominance of men in the various structures, institutions and processes. In the words of the President of the Republic of Somaliland, these are being taken to foster conditions for women's participation across all sectors of political and socio-economic life, including a deliberate policy, already in place, in favor of an incremental enrolment of female students in schools and all tertiary institutions.

f. There is a visibly emotional attachment to the reclaimed independence and a firm determination among the people of Somaliland not to return to the failed union with Somalia, whether or not recognition is granted. In the words of the President, *"should Africa and the international community insist on Somaliland re-establishing the union with Somalia, the leaders and people of Somaliland would "opt to fight again to preserve their independence. In fact, the Horn of Africa would be engulfed again in the old notions of a Greater Somalia and the pursuit of narrow-gauged national interests by countries in the region, with all the consequences befall the region."*

V. Observations and Recommendations

8. Going by the clear presentation and articulate demands of the authorities and people of Somaliland concerning their political, social and economic history, Somaliland has been made a "pariah region" by default. The Union established in 1960 brought enormous injustice and suffering to the people of the region. The fact that the "union between Somaliland and Somalia was never ratified" and also malfunctioned when it went into went into action from 1960 to 1990, makes Somaliland's search for recognition historically unique and self-justified in African political history. Objectively viewed, the case should not be linked to the notion of "opening a Pandora's box". As such, the AU should find a special method of dealing with this outstanding case.

9. The lack of recognition ties the hands of the authorities and people of Somaliland as they cannot effectively and

sustainably transact with the outside to pursue the reconstruction and development goals.

10. Whilst it remains a primary responsibility of the authorities and people of Somaliland to deploy efforts to acquire political recognition from the international community, the AU should be disposed to judge the case of Somaliland from an objective historical viewpoint and a moral angle vis-a-vis the aspirations of the people. Furthermore, given the acute humanitarian situation prevailing in Somaliland, the AU should mobilize financial resources to help alleviate the plight of the affected communities, especially those catering for the IDPs and Returnees.

11. Finally, given, also, the high potential for conflict between Mogadishu and Hargeysa, the AU should take steps to discuss critical issues in the relations between the two towns. That initiative should be taken the earliest possible

Appendix 6: Chronology of Somaliland direct elections

- ✓ 2021 Combined parliamentary and local council elections, sitting councils elected
- ✓ 2017 Presidential elections, current President, HE Muse Bihi Abdi elected
- ✓ 2010 Presidential elections, HE Ahmed Mahamed Mahamoud "Silaanyo" elected
- ✓ 2003 Presidential elections, HE Dahir Rayale Kahin elected.
- ✓ 2012 Local council elections, second local council direct elections elected.
- ✓ 2002 Local council elections, first local council direct elections elected.
- ✓ 2005 Parliamentary elections, first House of Representatives direct elections elected.

- ✓ 2001 Referendum on the constitution.

Appendix 7: Somaliland physical area and coastal line

Somaliland Map 1948 - Compiled and drawn by Directorate of Colonial Surveys Photolithographed and Printed in the UK

In the literature, it has been difficult to find an agreed measure of the coastal line and the area measurement of Somaliland, although it has been a defined administrative territory since 1884. Official colonial documents estimate the area of Somaliland as 60000 square miles (155,399 square km)[6]. Wiki commons says 137,000 square km. Anthony Kirk-Greene, On Crown Service (London: 1B Tauris, 1999) Table 2.8 says that in 1939 Somaliland covered an area of 68,000 square

---

[6] Openlibrary.org, *"Census of the British empire. 1901"*. Retrieved 25 September 2016.
https://archive.org/stream/cu31924030396067#page/n245/mode/2up

miles[7]. Similar thing happens when it comes to the coastal line of Somaliland. Official documents say 850km but recent measurements, which measured the actual coastal line as opposed to historic aerial or naval measurements, indicate that this figure may be an overestimate of true measure.

This is not a Somaliland only problem. In fact "determining the length of a country's coastline is not as simple as it first appears, as first considered by L. F. Richardson (1881-1953) and sometimes known as the Richardson effect" (Mandelbrot 1983). The scale of the ruler you use for the measurements determine the answer you get, and this what is called coastline paradox. "A shorter ruler measures more of the sinuosity of bays and inlets than a larger one, so the estimated length continues to increase as the ruler length decreases."

The coastline paradox is an interesting topic that comes back on the discussion nowadays because the new technology, in particularly satellite photography and measurements, allows more precision on measuring the coastline. The ground-breaking scientific paper *"How Long Is the Coast of Britain? Statistical Self-Similarity and*

---

[7] See Brock Millman, *"British Somaliland: An Administrative History, 1920-1960"*. 2013, Taylor & Francis

Fractional" by Benoit Mandelbrot in 1967 took as an example the west coast of Britain because "it looks like one of the most irregular coastline in the world." The paper stated, "Seacoast shapes are examples of highly involved curves such that each of their portion can be considered a reduced-scale image of the whole", and concluded, "speaking of a length for such figures is usually meaningless" [Mandelbrot, 1967]. Earlier studies indicated how the change of the scale and precision may effect the figures cited for geographical purposes, for instance Steinhaus writes ''the left bank of the Vistula, when measured with increased precision, would furnish lengths ten, a hundred or even a thousand times as great as the length read off the school map'' (Steinhaus, 1954).

There is huge variation of the measurement therefore in relation to the scale of the map. The Ordinance Survey measured and gave it to 11072 miles (or 17820km). For instance measurements in different scale show that the coastal line of the United Kingdom is calculated in 3960km when the scale of the map is 1:2,000,000. Researchers obtained that when doubled the scale in 1:1,000,000 the coastal line length becomes 4300, and when furthermore doubled the scale in 1:500,000, the length change to 4800 while if it still doubled, we have 6182Km and there is a difference of above 2000KM[8].

The new technology offers to us to be more precise. Using google map, for instant, we scaled down to 1:5000 which gives us a very detailed information and precision on the distance of the map. Delimiting borders in Somaliland, mainly in the eastern part also show some discrepancies on the available maps. The area is highly politicized recently and, in our measurement, we refer to the maps that has been produced before 1960 which are consistent with the borders as delimited by the 1897 treaty.

Measurements – Somaliland coastal line and area
Delimiting borders of Somaliland
Great Britain reached an agreement with France on the boundary between the respective territories they controlled on 2–9 February 1888. In order to determine the alignment of the British Somaliland–French Somaliland boundary, it was necessary to establish the exact starting point of the boundary on the Gulf of Aden.

---

[8] The "more or less" BBC Radio 4 program describes the Coastal Paradox (hear from minute 23 of the following podcast. [retrieved 15 October 2016].
http://www.bbc.co.uk/programmes/b07m7z12?imz_s=9c39flicm9a6193q4oqpprpea7

According to the Anglo–French agreement of 1888, the boundary began opposite the 'wells of Hadou, but these wells could not be located, so shortly after the agreement, British and French Government officials agreed that the northern point of the boundary was a short distance northeast of Loyada on the Gulf of Aden (approximately 11º 27' 55" N., 43º 15' 45" E.). The tripoint as to where these two boundaries would meet the Ethiopian boundary was decided in the 1930s on the basis of references to all the boundary agreements between the three countries. [See details in Jama Musse Jama (Ed.), "Time-line history of Somaliland", 2017].

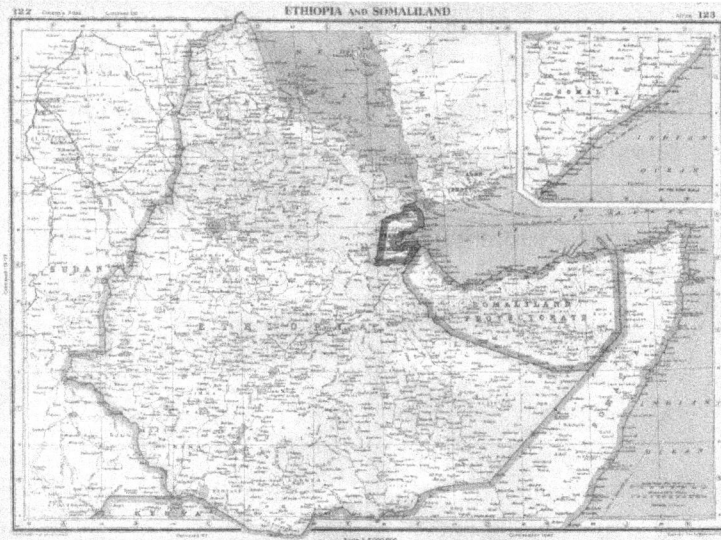

HORN OF AFRICA Ethiopia, French, British Somaliland Protectorate 1952

The Eastern Boundary of Somaliland was defined in the Anglo-Italian Protocol of 5 May 1894. It started at the intersection of the 8th Parallel North and Longitude 48 East, then moving diagonally northeast to the cross section of the 9th Parallel North and Longitude 49 East whereupon it follows that longitude straight to the Gulf of Aden. Here is how the Treaty described it: 'On reaching the 8th degree of north latitude the line follows that parallel as far as its intersection with the 48th degree of longitude east of Greenwich. It then runs to the intersection of the 9th degree of north latitude with the 49th degree of longitude east of Greenwich, and follows that meridian of longitude to the sea' (British Parliamentary Paper, Treaty Series No 1, 1894). Although the boundary between Ethiopia and Italian Somaliland has been in dispute, the tri-point between the three states at the intersection of 8° North, 48° East has not itself been the subject of any dispute. For further details, see details in Jama Musse Jama (Ed.), "Time-line history of Somaliland", 2017.

New Measurements – Somaliland coastal line

Coastal line: In (Jama Musse, 2017) it has been measured through google map with a scale of 50KM and found as 796.12KM without considering Sa'ad ad-Din islands. The frontiers between Somaliland and Ethiopia, between Somaliland and Djibouti, and between Somaliland and Somalia, is delimited by the Treaty (1897).

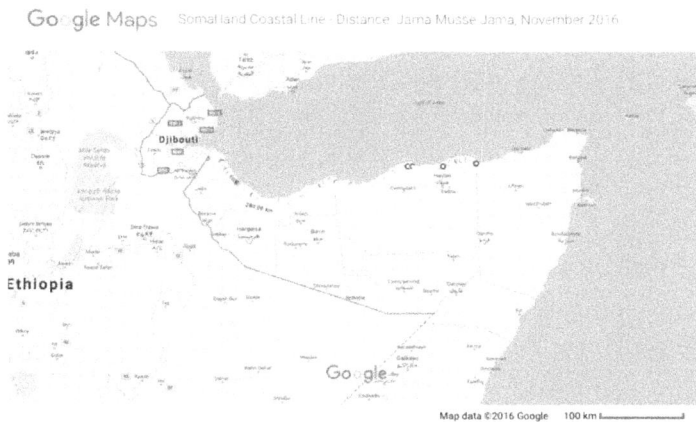

Digital coastal line

New Measurements – Somaliland area

Area: In (Jama Musse, 2017) it has been measured through google map with a scale of 50KM and found as 169,226.89KM^2 (65,338.87 square miles) without considering Sa'ad ad-Din islands.

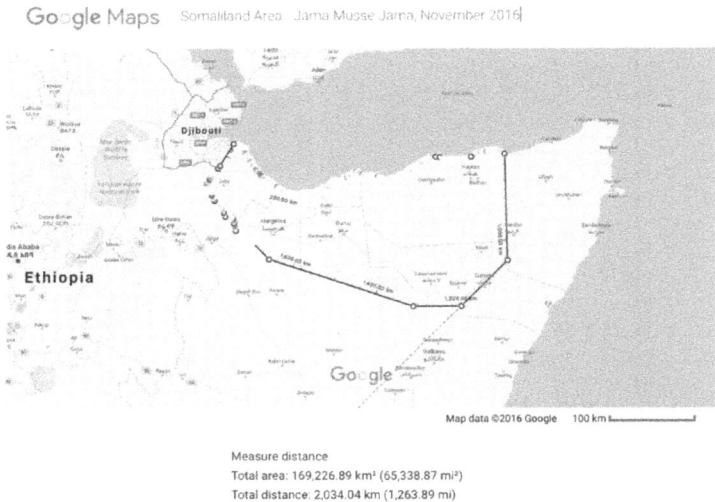

Digital - Somaliland Area

Appendix 8: President Muse Bihi Abdi Speech in Djibouti

President Muse Bihi Abdi addressed 14th June 2020 in Djibouti on Somaliland-Somalia Relations at a Consultation Summit in Djibouti. The text has been transcribed from the audio recording publicly available online.

Your Excellency, Ismail Omer Gelleh, The President of the Republic of Djibouti;
Your Excellency, Dr. Abiye Ahmed, The Prime Minister of the Federal Democratic Republic of Ethiopia;
Your Excellency, Mohamed Abdillahi Farmajo, President of Somalia;
Your Excellency, Hassan Ali Khayre, The Prime Minister of Somalia;
Representative of the Chairperson of the African Union (if they are here);
Your Excellency, Dr. Warkneh Gebeyehu, The Executive Secretary of IGAD;
Your Excellency, Donald Yamamoto, The U.S. Ambassador to Somalia and Somaliland;
Excellencies, distinguished guests; ladies and gentlemen; all protocols observed, good afternoon:

Mr. President and Chairman as well,

First and foremost, let me say that it's a great pleasure to be here with you today, and to participate in the continuation of the dialogue between Somaliland and

Somalia. Allow me to extend my sincere appreciation to the regional, continental, and international community for your presence here today to discuss a topic of great importance to the Horn of Africa.

Allow me to further thank His Excellency, President Ismail Guelleh and the people of Djibouti for their warm and brotherly hospitality in welcoming us in this beautiful country. Though we may be separated by land and sea, nothing will diminish the importance for -- the important role you all play, and will continue to play, in your efforts to bring peace and stability to the African continent.

The region is suffering from a combination of unprecedented challenges, which range from the COVID-19 to environmental and socio-economic issues. Regional cooperation and hegemony is urgently required to steward the vulnerable to a more prosperous and stable future.

Restarting of these mediation talks with international support is an important factor in securing a more sustainable future in the fulfilment of [the onerous] and worthy duty of building a safe, secure, and stable relationship for the people for Somaliland and Somalia.

Excellencies, allow me to stress the current phase that we are entering is crucial in shaping the future -- the future bilateral relationships between our two neighboring countries, regional stability, and a sustainable and prosperous future for the Horn of Africa. However daunting or important such a task is, I remain confident and optimistic that through our and your attention, commitment, hard work, and dedication we will be able to contribute to the peace and security landscape across the continent of Africa.

Excellences, allow me to present a brief historical background on how we got to where we are today. Republic of Somaliland received its independence from the United Kingdom on 26th June 1960. Notification of that independence was duly registered with the United Nations and 35 countries recognized Somaliland. Somaliland voluntarily united with Somalia on 1st July, 1960 to form the Somali Republic. The union was not legally binding, as the Act of Union was never formally signed. Therefore, the unification effort fell short of the requirements mandated by domestic and international law.

From the beginning, the union malfunctioned as Somaliland people were hugely oppressed. The people of Somaliland expressed their displeasure with the union by overwhelmingly voting against the new constitution in the referendum held in 1961 and followed full-scale struggle against the Somali Republic. This resulted in the collapse of the Somali Republic in 1991 and the restoration of the independence of -- of the Republic of Somaliland, 18th May 1991.

Since restoring our independence, Somaliland with its scarce resources, and with limited international support, has embarked on a steady, incremental, and progressive agenda of conflict resolution, peace building and state building, and established good governance and functioning government institutions. We conducted a constitutional referendum in which 97 percent of Somalilanders voted to support the constitution and the independence of Somaliland. During that period Somaliland has made rounds of multiparty free and fair elections, including three rounds of presidential elections, two rounds of local council elections, and a parliamentary election. Republic of Somaliland created a conducive environment that enabled a thriving private sector and an in-flow of international investment. Somaliland has played an important role in the peace and security of the region and has been a reliable partner in the fight against terrorism, piracy, human trafficking, money laundering, and other forms of organized crimes.

Unfortunately, instead of appreciating all those efforts and contributions made by the Somaliland people for the last 30 years, Somalia was in a constant war against the development of Somaliland -- economically, security-wise, investment-wise, and this deepened the mistrust and animosity between the two countries. Ever since Somaliland entered hastily into a voluntary union with Somalia, the -- the Somaliland people have been at the receiving end of injustice, discrimination, and state sponsored genocide at -- at the hands of the Somalia government.

Evidence of the widespread war crimes committed against the people of Somaliland has been fully documented by the United Nations Special Rapporteur for human rights, and a forensic team from Physicians for Human Rights, and Somaliland War Crimes Commission.

The acts of genocide perpetrated by the Siad Barre regime are -- are memorialized in more than 200 mass graves in our country. The mass graves, which are still being unearthed, will forever testify to the crimes against humanity committed by the government of Somalia against the people of Somaliland.

Therefore, in approaching the present situation in Somaliland and Somalia, it's necessary to have a proper regard to the past and learn lessons from it. The legacy of oppression against the people of Somaliland cannot be easily swept away. Rather, they must be acknowledged and taken into account when considering Somaliland people's right to self-determination and independence.

The case for Somaliland independence is unique. This fact is also acknowledged by the AU mission to Somaliland in 2005 that concluded the situation was sufficiently "unique and self-justified in African political history" that "the case should not be linked to the notion of opening a Pandora's box.'" It recommended that the African Union *"should find a special method of dealing with this outstanding case" at the earliest possible date.*

Furthermore, the 2005 African Union fact mission to Somaliland reported that the "plethora of problems confronting Somaliland are in part the legacy of a political union with Somalia, which malfunctioned and brought destruction and ruin thereby overburdening the population" of Somaliland. Somaliland's claim to independence depends on part upon its circumstance, including its brief, but legal, period of independence in 1960 -- its claim to recognized international borders relating to that period. As can be surmised from Somaliland's case is unique and demands unique solution. It does not create precedent for other unresolved conflicts in Africa or elsewhere.

Somaliland's legal case for independence is in conformity with international law. Somaliland satisfies the statehood criteria as set out in the Montevideo convention of 1933. Somaliland fulfils the conditions set out in article 4(b) of the Constitutive Act of the African Union which enshrines respect of borders existing on the achievement of independence since Somaliland borders correspond to those received upon independence from the Great Britain.

Somaliland is fully aware that in the African context, the exercise of the right to self-determination is linked to the principle of respect for pre-existing boundaries [uti possidetis juris]. Somaliland's case for independence involves resorting borders it possessed both as a colonial entity and as an independent state.

Between 1991 and 2000, the Organization of African Unity consented to the break-up of two other unions. In 1989, Senegal opted to terminate the seven-year merger with Gambia as Senigambia federation and 1993 Eretria formerly seceded from Ethiopia. Furthermore, in supporting the comprehensive peace agreement signed in 2005 and subsequently independence of South Sudan and its admission to the African Union, the African Union has accepted the break-up of Sudan -- Southern Sudan.

The International Court of Justice in its legal opinion on Kosovo declared in 10 to 4 vote that the declaration of independence of Kosovo of the 17th of February 19 -- 2008...did not violate general international law because the international law provides no prohibition on declaration of independence.

Furthermore, the Arbitration Commission of the Peace Conference for Yugoslavia produced a series of opinions on the validity of new states' claim to independence and conditions for recognition. The Commission determined, inter alia, the break-up of Yugoslavia was as case of dissolution rather than secession.

Somaliland's pursuit of independence is not a case of secession but rather dissolution of voluntary union between two independent states. A number of African Union member states are also the product of a failed union: Mali, Senegal, Gambia and Egypt have all withdrawn from unions with their borders intact. The African Union has also accepted the independence of territories that never previously enjoyed full sovereignty.

Following the failure of the unity government, Republic of Somaliland exercised its inherent right to self-determination which are consistent with the preamble of UN 1948 Universal Declaration of Human Rights. Somaliland has long argued that Somali Republic was two united countries. The failure of the unity government provided adequate ground for the restoration of our independence.

We believe in that the key to sustainable and peaceful future lies in the honest and sincere dialogue between Somaliland and Somalia under the auspice of a neutral and impartial international mediation mechanism and a guarantor.

Somaliland remains committed to peaceful co-existence with Somalia. However, Somaliland insists in that the dialogue should be a two-state process with a substantive agenda that addresses the core issues of the dispute. Today, how can we proceed to this dialogue if the previously signed agreements in London, Istanbul, Accra, and Djibouti were not implemented yet? We cordially propose that a serious mediation mechanism *and a guarantor should be in place for this new round of dialogue.*

We thank Somalia for their sincere apology for the horrors of yesteryear committed in Somaliland. The current generation of Somalia was of course not responsible for what the previous generations did but its acknowledgement of the wrongdoings of the previous generation is significant and heartfelt appreciated by all Somalilanders.

But with acknowledgment also comes responsibility -- responsibility for the damage that horror caused. Words are not enough. Again, words are not enough. The horror of the past requires more than words -- it requires actions. The act of recognizing and supporting the independence of Somaliland would go a long way to heal the wounds of the past and enable our two states to embrace each other in our independent but closely interwoven futures.

I am confident that we can build a bright future together as brotherly, neighboring nations and for our own people and our region.

Thank you very much.

DEPARTMENT OF STATE
FOR THE PRESS

JUNE 27, 1960   NO. 357

There follows the text of Secretary Herter's message to the Council of Ministers of Somaliland on the occasion of the independence of that nation on June 26, 1960:

"June 26, 1960

Their Excellencies,

Council of Ministers of Somaliland,

Hargeisa.

Your Excellencies:

I extend my best wishes and congratulations on the achievement of your independence. This is a noteworthy milestone in your history, and it is with pleasure that I send my warmest regards on this happy occasion.

/s/

Christian A. Herter
Secretary of State,
United States of America"

. . .

This is the text of Secretory Herter's message to the Council of Ministers of Somaliland on the occasion of the Independence of the nation on 26 June 1960.

References

Africa Union, *Resumé: AU Fact-Finding Mission to Somaliland (30 April to 4 May 2005)*. Reported entirely here in Appendix 5.

Africom, 2022, U.S. Africa Command Press Release, May 12, 2022, available on www.africom.mil (accessed May 22nd, 2022).

Africa intelligence, 1999. SOMALILAND: Egal's US contacts, The Indian Ocean Newsletter, 09/10/1999.

Bradbury, M., 2008, Becoming Somaliland, Oxford: James Currey.

Brock Millman, *"British Somaliland: An Administrative History, 1920-1960"*. 2013, Taylor & Francis

Christopher Clapham, Holger Hansen, Jeffrey Herbst, J. Peter Pham, Patrick Mazimhaka, Susan Schulman, and Greg Mills, African Game Changer? The Consequences of Somaliland's International (Non) Recognition, Brenthurst Foundation Discussion Paper, June 2011.

ICG, Somaliland: Time for African Union Leadership Crisis Group Africa Report No 110, 2006.

Jama Musse, J. (ed)., 2019, Somaliland: A political history. Pisa. Ponte Invisibile.

Jhazbhay, Iqbal D. 2009. Somaliland: An African Struggle for Nationhood and International Recognition. Johannesburg: Institute for Global Dialogue and South African Institute of International Affairs.

Mandelbrot, B. B. "How Long Is the Coast of Britain." Ch. 5 in The Fractal Geometry of Nature. New York: W. H. Freeman, pp. 25-33, 1983.

Mills, G.; Githongo, J.; Steenhuisen, J.; Haji, Abbasali; Mwanawasa, Chipokota; Biti, T. (4 June 2021). "Somaliland: The Power of Democracy". Royal United Services Institute.

J. Peter Pham, "The Somaliland Exception: Lessons on Postconflict State Building from the Part of the Former Somalia That Works," Marine Corps University Journal, Spring 2012.

David H. Shinn, 2002, Somaliland: The Little Country that Could. Africa Notes, November 2002.

Steinhaus, Hugo (1954). "Length, shape and area". Colloquium Mathematicum. 3 (1): 1–13. doi:10.4064/cm-3-1-1-13.

UNPW, A Shadow on Tomorrow's Dreams: Somaliland's Struggle for Statehood, 2016, Unrepresented Nations and Peoples Workshop Lewis & Clark Law School.

Walls, M., 2014, A Somali Nation-state: History, culture and Somaliland's political transition. 2nd edition (Pisa: Ponte Invisibile)

Walls, M., Stevens, M., Sullivan, K., Fradgley, S., & Howell, D. 2021. Limited International Election Observation Mission - Somaliland House of Representatives and Local Council Elections, 31 May 2021. London: DPU, UCL.

Walls, M. Kibble, S., Swerves on the road: Report by international election observers on the 2012 local elections in Somaliland (Progressio, London, 2013).

General reading on Somaliland

Abdi Sheikh Abdi (1993) Divine madness. Zed books Ltd.

Ahmed, H. Adam (2013) Media Industry in Somaliland: The Current Practice and Its Law and Other Regulatory Frameworks. Available online.

Ahmed, H. Adam (2007) "Somaliland media: an overview and introduction". www.Somalilandlaw.com
Ansari, H. (2004). The Infidel Within: Muslims in Britain Since 1800. C. Hurst & Co. Publishers.

Battersby, H.F. Prevost (1914) Richard Corfield of Somaliland. Arnlod.

Bradbury, M. et al, (2003) Somaliland: Choosing Politics over Violence", Review of African Political Economy, Vol. 30, No. 97, pp. 455 – 478.

Bradbury, Mark, (2008) Becoming Somaliland. African issues.

Briggs, P. (2012). Somaliland with Addis Ababa & Eastern Ethiopia. Bradt Travel Guides.

Brockett, A.M. (1969) The British Somaliland Protectorate to 1905 PhD dissertation, Lincoln college, Oxford.

Bryden, M. (2000) Decentralized Governance in Somaliland: Observations from the WSP Perspective. WSP/Somaliland Centre for Peace and Development. Somaliland.

Bulhan, Hussein, 2008, *Politics of Cain, one hundred years of crises in Somali politics and society*. Tayosan International Publishing.
Burton, Richard (1987) *First footsteps in East Africa or, An Exploration of Harar*. Dover Publication, Inc. New York.

Cali, J. Maxamed (Faroole) Halgankii& Hal-Adaygii Faarax Oomar (1871-1949), 2014, Sagaljet

Cassanelli, L. (1982), The Shaping of the Somali Society, Restructuring the History of the Pastoral People, 1600-1900, University of Pennsylvania Press.

Collier, P. (2008). The Bottom Billion: Why the Poorest Countries are Failing and What Can Be Done About It. Oxford University Press.

Commonwealth Digest, Volume 4 (1963). Somali Students in Britain Demand for Education in English (section).

Communities and Local Government, (2009) The Somali Muslim Community in England Understanding Muslim Ethnic Communities.

Cotran, Eugene (1963) Legal Problems arising out of the formation of the Somali Republic. The International and comparative Law quarterly, Vol.12, No.3 (July 1963) pp 1010-1026, Cambridge University Press.

Day, K. and White, P.E. (2002). Choice or circumstance: the UK as the location of asylum applications by Bosnian and Somali refugees. GeoJournal, 56 (1), 15-26.

Drysdale, J. (2000) Stoics without Pillows; A way forward for the Somalilanders. Haan Associates.

Dualeh, H. (2002) Search for a New Somali Identity. Printed in the Republic of Kenya.

Eubank, N. (2010) "Peace-Building without External Assistance: Lessons from Somaliland". CGD Working Paper 198. Washington, D.C: Center for Global Development.

Farah, A.Y and I.M. Lewis. (1993) Somalia: Roots of Reconciliation. Peace Making Endeavours of Contemporary Lineage Leaders: A Survey of Grassroots Peace Conferences in "Somaliland". London: ActionAid.

Fryer, P. (1984). Staying Power: The History of Black People in Britain. The University of Alberta.

Gibney, J.M and Hansen, A. R. (2005) Immigration and Asylum: From1900 to the Present, Volume 1

Gilliat-Ray, S. (2010) Muslims in Britain, U. Cambridge University Press.

Gorka, H. (2011) Somaliland: A Walk on Thin Ice. Published by KAS International Reports.

Gundel, J. (2002) U. International Migration, 40 (5), 255 281.

Hall, D. (1961) Somaliland's Last Year as a Protectorate, African Affairs, no. 238. pp. 26–37.

Hammond, L. (2010) Obligated to Give: Remittance and the Maintenance of Transnational Networks Between

Somalis at Home and Abroad. Bildhaan: An International Journal of Somali Studies, Volume 10.

Harper, J. M. (2012) Getting Somalia Wrong? Faith, War and Hope in a Shattered State. Zed Books.

Hofmann, Steven. R. (2002) „The Divergent Paths of Somalia and Somaliland: The Effects of Centralization on Indigenous Institutions of Self-Governance and Post-Collapse Reconciliation and State-Building", Institutional Analysis and Development.

Human Rights Watch. (2009) Somaliland: 'Hostage to Peace' – Threats to Human Rights and Democracy in Somaliland. New York: Human Rights Watch.

ICG 2006 Somaliland: Time for AU Leadership, Africa Report No 110.

Laitin, David and Samatar, Said (1987) Somalia: Nation in Search of a State Dartmouth Publishing Co Ltd

Lewis, I.M. (2002), A modern history of the Somali: nation and state in the Horn of Africa, (4th ed), James Currey Publishers, Oxford.

Lewis, I. M., "Lessons from Somaliland: appropriate technology for Peace processes". Available online.

Lewis, I M. (1994) Blood and Bone: The Call of Kinship in Somali Society, Lawrenceville, N.J: The Red Sea Press.

Lewis, M. (2011) Understanding Somalia and Somaliland: Culture, History, Society.Columbia University Press.

Lindley, A. (2010) The Early Morning Phone Call: Somali Refugees' Remittances. Studies in forced migration, Volume 28, Berghahn Books.

Lyons, T. and Mandavill, P. (2011) (ed). Politics from Afar: Transnational Diasporas and Networks. Hurst Publishers.

Nasir, M.A. (2011) "Searching for Identity: Examining Somaliland's quest for Recognition". International Journal of Research and Sustainable Development.

Nur, AH (April 2011)- short briefing paper: Egypt, Israel, Ghana and Libya extended diplomatic recognition to Somaliland?

Pegg, Scott and Kolsto, Pal (2015) Somaliland: Dynamics of internal legitimacy and (lack of) external Sovereignty.

Renders, Marleen (2012) Considering Somaliland: State building with traditional leaders and institutions. Published by Brill, Netherlands.

Samatar, I. A. (1989) The State and Rural Transformation in Northern Somalia, 1884-1986).

Touval (Weltmann), Saadia (1963) SOMALI NATIONALISM, Oxford University Press: London

Trunji, Mohamed (2015) Somalia: The untold history 1941-1969

Walls, M., 2009, 'The Emergence of a Somali State: Building Peace from Civil War in Somaliland', African Affairs, 108(432): 371-389

Walls, Michael (2014) A Somali nation-state: history, culture, and Somaliland's political transition

Walls, M. and S. Kibble, 2010, 'Beyond Polarity: Negotiating a Hybrid State in Somaliland', Africa Spectrum, 45(1): 31-56

Zartman, William (1995) Collapsed States: The Disintegration and Restoration of Legitimate Authority

WSP International. Rebuilding Somaliland: Issues and Possibilities (Red Sea Press, Lawrenceville NJ/Asmara: 2005).

The Brenthurst Foundation, African Game Changer? The Consequences of Somaliland's International (Non) Recognition – Discussion Paper 2011/05,

Index

About the author

Jama Musse Jama is an ethnomathematician with a PhD in African Studies specialising in Computational Linguistics of African Languages. He has authored and edited several books. Dr Jama is known for his research on traditional African games and their potential for use within formal education. A cultural activist, historical researcher and a preserver of Somali oral histories, Jama Musse is the founder of Hargeysa Cultural Centre and the influential Hargeysa International Book Fair. In 2018 he was the hosts of the 13th International Congress of Somali Studies International Association in Hargeysa. Dr Jama has research associate position in UCL, and in early 2022, he has been nominated as Senior European Affairs Advisor to the President. Dr Jama Musse Jama can be reached through twitter.com/jamamusse.

Other books authored or edited:
- Qaraami: the fading melody of Somali Classical Music, 2023. Ponte Invisibile: Hargeysa.
- *Hummaagyada Naxariista Leh ee ku Jira Heesaha Kalgacalka*, 2023 (With Xafsa Cumar Sh Cabdillaahi), Ponte Invisibile: Hargeysa.
- Galxiddigaale Walk - from Laasgeel to Bullaxaar, Somaliland, Ponte Invisibile ed., Hargeysa, 2021
- Somaliland – a political history, Ponte Invisibile ed., Pisa, 2017
- *Cittadinanza è Partecipazione*, Bianca & Volta, Trieste, 2013

- Maxamed Ibraahim Warsame "Hadraawi" – the man and the poet, (edited), Ponte Invisibile, Pisa, 2013
- Maxamed Xaashi Dhamac "Gaarriye", Life and Poems, (edited), Ponte Invisibile, Pisa, 2012
- Somaliland – the way forward, vol. 1., Jama Musse Jama (edited), Pisa, 2011
- Essays in Honour of Muuse Galaal, Jama Musse Jama (edited), Pisa, 2011
- *Superkeey – la leucemia non è un gioco*, ETS, Pisa, 2010.
- *Gobannimo Bilaash maaha* (freedom is not free), Jama Musse Jama, Ponte Invisibile, 2007
- A Note on My Teachers Group: News report of an injustice. Ponte Invisibile, 2003
- Shax: the preferred game of our camel-herders. SUN MOON LAKE, 2000, Rome.
- *Layli Goobalay: Variante Somala del Gioco Nazionale Africano*. Ponte Invisibile, 2002.

The mission in pictures

Randomly selected photos from the mission.

Notes for knowing more about the mission:

_____

_____

_____

_____

_____

_____

_____

_____

_____

_____

_____

_____

_____

_____

_____

_____

_____

_____

_____

_____

_____

_____

_____

_____

_____

_____

_____

_____

_____

_____

_____

_____

_____

_____

_____

_____

_____

_____

_____

_____

_____

_____

_____

_____

_____

_____

_____

_____

_____

_____

Milton Keynes UK
Ingram Content Group UK Ltd.
UKHW020652081023
430166UK00008B/54

9 788888 934754